LEGO

POCKET BOOK OF POWERS

By Len Forgione

Scholastic Inc.

MAP OF KNIGHTON

Take note, knights-in-training! There are many NEXO Powers that you can use to make sure you're at your best when fighting the baddies. You can find a handy, helpful map of Knighton in the front of this guide. Be sure to consult the map for help locating NEXO Powers (wherever they may be) as you journey across the land battling Jestro's monstrous min-ions. Remember, you might not be able to find all these Powers at the same time—some may become active later in the year. The more NEXO Powers you have, the better chances you'll have of defeating Jestro and Monstrox once and for all! Good luck to you!

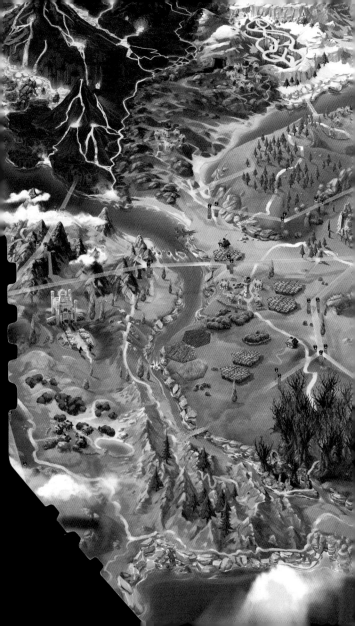

LOCATIONS

- ► **LEGO Club Magazine** (online and print)
- ► **LEGO.com** (webisodes and mini movies)
- ► **LEGOLAND Theme Parks**
- ► **LEGO NEXO KNIGHTS** extended line (clothes, clocks, lights, trading cards, and more)
- ► **LEGO NEXO KNIGHTS Books**
- ► **LEGO NEXO KNIGHTS** Products (building sets, minifigures, and more)
- ► **LEGO NEXO KNIGHTS** TV Show
  - ► **LEGO store promotions** and events
    - ► **Merlok 2.0 App**

LETTER FROM MERLOK 2.0

Hello, young knights-in-training, and welcome to the *Pocket Book of Powers*! This is our attempt to catalog all of the NEXO Powers we're aware of (and some that should never be used!).

NEXO Powers are old magic spells digitized into a computer system. From my OS (operating system) here, I can upload these Powers to the shields that our knights carry with them.

The NEXO KNIGHTS team uses their NEXO Powers to fight Jestro and his evil buddies. Against these magical monsters, regular weapons are useless! But with the help of the NEXO Powers, you have more than a fighting chance—you can destroy the bad guys and defend Knighton! Your shield is the key—it functions as a traditional shield would, but it is much more than that. It contains a digital uplink with a Wi-Fi interface. This is how I can upload digital NEXO Powers to your shield. Hold your shields high and feel the energy flow into them and through your armor. You'll get a cool weapon, extra strength, sometimes even a banana bomb—anything you need to finish the fight! Experiment with the NEXO Powers to find the right one for the job. You can do it!

Don't be afraid to try all of the Powers out and find out what each one does. As you find new Powers, scan them in and see how they work on the battlefield. Powers can be found in many different places, so make sure you look far and wide to find them. If it's not the right Power for that particular enemy, you'll know pretty quickly—it will have little effect on them. But when you hit on the right Power, you'll see the damage it does to Jestro's minions!

Oh, and before I forget: Some of the NEXO Powers are purely for offensive purposes, meant for attacking the bad guys and monsters, and some are defensive—they'll protect you from harm! Others will support you and your team as you venture out onto the battlefield. You'll learn which Powers to use at the appropriate times for maximum effect. Was that everything?

All right, now that we've gotten that out of the way—good luck to you, young knights-in-training. There are many dangerous creatures afoot in Knightonia now (reminds me of the old days), but you're more than up to the challenge! Take up arms, power up your vehicle, and use your NEXO Powers to defend Knighton and the good citizens that live here! Your friends and families are counting on you, and King and Queen Halbert send their royal thanks. Remember, we're here to support you, too.

Good luck!
Merlock 2.0

Glossary of Abbreviations

AoE: Area of Effect
AP: Attack Power
DoT: Damage over Time
DPS: Damage per Second
HP: Hit Points or Health Points
N/A: Not Applicable

ACHILLES' HEEL

Description: Stomp your opponents with a big giant foot!

Category: Offensive

Element: Armor

Type: Area of Effect (AoE), Weapon Enhancer

Damage: Base: 100 HP, 500% AP.

Effect: Flatten and stun enemies.

Location: TV Show

*"Taste de agony
of de feet!"*
—AXL

ADRENALINE RUSH

Description: Your knight receives a surge of energy and health!

Category: Supportive

Element: Electricity

Type: Self

Damage: N/A

Effect: Regenerate 4% of total health per second and increase movement and speed by 10%.

Location: In-store, LEGO.COM

AGENT OF AWESOME

Description: For ten seconds, zoom into your opponent and do some damage!

Category: Offensive

Element: Magic

Type: Area of Effect (AoE), Weapon Enhancer

Damage: Base: 50 HP, 250% AP.

Effect: Knock back.

Location: TV Show

AIR PORTAL

Description: Zap your enemies through a portal and watch them crash back onto the ground. Follow them through to execute a smashing attack that deals extra damage!

Category: Offensive

Element: Magic

Type: Area of Effect (AoE), Weapon Enhancer

Damage: Base: 75 HP, 300% AP when landing.

Effect: N/A

Location: Products

ALGEBRA GAMBLE

Description: Form a triangle around your enemies for massive damage!

Category: Offensive

Element: Magic

Type: Area of Effect (AoE), Weapon Enhancer

Damage: Base: 75 HP, 400% AP upon landing.

Effect: Pull enemies toward the middle of the vortex; knock upward.

Location: TV Show

ALLIANCE OF THE FORTREX

Description: Summon the mighty Fortrex to help you in battle! Fires two rotating mini-cannons at random enemies.

Category: Offensive

Element: Armor

Type: Area of Effect (AoE)

Damage: Base: 50 HP, 200% AP (x6 shots).

Effect: Increase defense.

Location: TV Show, In-store

ALPHA DRILL

Description: A huge drill explodes out of the ground, damaging enemies in a swirling storm! The drill follows you around and does damage when it disappears back underground.

Category: Offensive

Element: Weapon

Type: Area of Effect (AoE), Weapon Enhancer

Damage: 25 HP, 150% AP/second.

Effect: Enemies are slowly dragged toward the drill; push enemies back when the drill pushes in the ground.

Location: In-store

ANVIL OF TROUBLE

Description: A giant hammer hits a massive anvil in the midst of battle and shrapnel is launched in every direction.

Category: Offensive

Element: Weapon

Type: Area of Effect (AoE), Weapon Enhancer

Damage: Base: 100 HP; Anvil Landing: 300% AP. Anvil Explosion: 700% AP each.

Effect: N/A

Location: Products

ARMADILLO SHELTER

Description: Dome resembling an armadillo appears around the knight, greatly reducing damage taken.

Category: Defensive

Element: Animal

Type: Area of Effect (AoE), Weapon Enhancer

Damage: N/A

Effect: Damage reduced by 30%. Heal the knight for 4% of their max HP.

Location: TV show

ARROW STRIKE

Description: Direct a volley of poisonous arrows toward your foes.

Category: Offensive

Element: Weapon

Type: Area of Effect (frontal)

Damage: Base: 75 HP; DoT 25 HP; 100% AP/second.

Effect: Each arrow hit has a 20% chance to inflict a poison effect on the target, dealing an additional 50% AP/second.

Location: Products

ARCTIC BREATH

Description: Blast your enemies with an ice storm beam from your NEXO Shield. Control the beam by moving your knight.

Category: Offensive

Element: Ice

Type: Area of Effect (AoE), Weapon Enhancer

Damage: Base: 50 HP, 200% AP/second

Effect: Enemies slowed by 30%.

Location: Products

ATOMIC ACORN

Description: Launch an atomic acorn on the battlefield!

Category: Offensive

Element: Food

Type: Area of Effect (AoE), Weapon Enhancer

Damage: Base: 150 HP, 1500% AP on elite/boss monsters.

Effect: Destroy all non-elite/boss monsters. Knight loses 33% of health.

Location: LEGOLAND, In-store

AVENGING ULTRA ARMOR

Description: Your knight calls upon the power of the earth to add rocks to their armor, reducing damage received.

Category: Defensive

Element: Armor

Type: Self

Damage: N/A

Effect: Reduce damage received by 75%, immunity to stun, reduce movement speed by 30%.

Location: TV Show

BACKFIRE

Description: Your knight creates three protective spheres that float around him. When the knight is hit, a sphere is consumed and the enemy takes damage.

Category: Defensive

Element: Weapon

Type: Self

Damage: Base: 75 HP.

Effect: The next five attacks to hit your knight deal damage to your enemies equal to 300% of their damage.

Location: Products, LEGO.COM

BACKLASH LIGHTNING

Description: The knight's shield emits a devastating lightning bolt that bounces among enemies up to five times.

Category: Offensive

Element: Electricity

Type: Line (through)

Damage: Base: 100 HP; Target #1 = 500% AP, Targets #2–5 = 250% AP.

Effect: Hit up to five targets.

Location: Products, In-store

BAD BOILS

Description: Pop random blobs of goo on the ground to do damage.

Category: Offensive

Element: Poison

Type: Area of Effect (AoE), Weapon Enhancer

Damage: Base: 50 HP, DoT 25 HP, 500% AP (small AoE), 100% AP/second.

Effect: Both knights and enemies can walk on them to trigger an explosion, but knights won't take damage.

Location: LEGO Club Magazine, In-store

BANANA BOMBS

Description: Your knight places a banana trap on the ground. When an enemy approaches, the banana explodes, dealing damage to the enemy and healing your knight.

Category: Offensive

Element: Food

Type: Trap

Damage: Base: 100 HP, 500% AP.

Effect: Knight recovers 15% of their total health.

Location: Products

"Bananas? Delicious! I shall make ze dessert with zem."

—Chef Éclair

BATTLE CRY

Description: Unleash a damaging sound wave at your enemies!

Category: Offensive

Element: Sound

Type: Area of Effect (AoE), Weapon Enhancer

Damage: N/A

Effect: Stun surrounding enemies. Heals knight for 25% of their Max HP.

Location: Products

BEAM JUMP

Description: Your knight teleports and strikes every enemy on-screen!

Category: Offensive

Element: Armor

Type: Area of Effect (AoE), Weapon Enhancer

Damage: Base: 100 HP, 500% AP on each enemy.

Effect: N/A

Location: Extended line, Products

BEAR CLAWS

Description: Your knight summons the might of the bear and deals damage to multiple enemies.

Category: Offensive

Element: Animal

Type: Area of Effect (AoE), Weapon Enhancer

Damage: Base: 100 HP, 1000% AP on each enemy.

Effect: 2 hits every second, 1 hit per target.

Location: In-store

BEAR THE BRUNT

Description: Let loose a giant roar that knocks back all enemies. Can move while using this NEXO Power.

Category: Offensive

Element: Animal

Type: Area of Effect (AoE), Weapon Enhancer

Damage: Base: 25 HP, 275% AP.

Effect: Five consecutive shock waves are released, knocking back enemies to the edge of the screen.

Location: In-store

BEARDED BALLERINA

Description: A bearded hipster lady Squirebot emerges from a beam of light with dual swords!

Category: Offensive

Element: Sound

Type: Area of Effect (AoE), Weapon Enhancer

Damage: Base: 50 HP, 200% AP.

Effect: This bearded 'bot deals damage and knocks back your enemies while dancing around with swords.

Location: Products

BEETLE BOMB

Description: Summon a large beetle that swarms your enemies and explodes!

Category: Offensive

Element: Insect

Type: Line (through)

Damage: Base: 100 HP, 1125% AP.

Effect: N/A

Location: Products, In-store

BIG TURKEY

Description: Unleash a giant turkey on your foes—no artificial flavors added!

Category: Offensive

Element: Bird

Type: Area of Effect (AoE), Weapon Enhancer

Damage: N/A

Effect: Spawns turkey legs. Heals your knight for 10% of their max HP for each turkey leg you pick up.

Location: In-store

BLACK LOBSTER CLAWS

Description: Lure your enemies into a "Lobster Trap" where two giant lobster claws smash into the ground.

Category: Offensive

Element: Animal

Type: Area of Effect (AoE), Weapon Enhancer

Damage: Base: 100 HP, 300% AP for each swing (three pairs of swings for a total of six hits).

Effect: Repeats three times per use.

Location: Extended line

BLADE OF BRAVERY

Description: Glowing energy surrounds your knight's weapon. Heal a little each time you strike an enemy.

Category: Offensive

Element: Animal

Type: Area of Effect (AoE), Weapon Enhancer

Damage: N/A

Effect: Restore health equal to 15% of damage done.

Location: Merlok 2.0 App

BLAST MASK

Description: A welder's mask covers your knight's entire body. Stun and knock back your enemies with this NEXO Power.

Category: Offensive

Element: Armor

Type: Area of Effect (AoE), Weapon Enhancer

Damage: Base: 50 HP, 500% AP.

Effect: Knock upward, stun.

Location: Products

BOMB BLAST

Description: A bomb falls on the battlefield and explodes upon landing, engulfing your enemies in flames.

Category: Offensive

Element: Explosion

Type: Area of Effect (AoE), Weapon Enhancer

Damage: Base: 100 HP, DoT 25 HP, 750% AP.

Effect: Flames 100% AP/second.

Location: Products

BONE SHAKER

Description: Rush in an enemy's direction and slam into them. They will fly backward into other enemies in their path, knocking them all down.

Category: Offensive

Element: Armor

Type: Area of Effect (AoE), Weapon Enhancer

Damage: Base: 100 HP, 1200% AP.

Effect: First target impact effect—heavy knock back. Second target damage—half of damage first enemy took. Second target impact effect—smaller knock back.

Location: In-store

BONKERS BEANS

Description: Delicious beans fall from the sky to a random location. Your knight can feast on them to increase speed and health regeneration.

Category: Supportive

Element: Plant

Type: Self

Damage: N/A

Effect: Increase movement speed by 25%. Regenerate 2% of max health per second. Refreshes when you pick another bean!

Location: Products, TV Show

BOOMERANG

Description: Unleash a projectile that hits your enemy twice—once on its way to the enemy, and once on its way back to your knight.

Category: Offensive

Element: Weapon

Type: Area of Effect (AoE), Weapon Enhancer

Damage: Base: 75 HP, 625% AP + 625% AP (boomerang back and forth).

Effect: N/A

Location: In-store, Products

BOOMSTICK

Description: Your knight wields a powerful "stick" in charge mode.

Category: Offensive

Element: Plant

Type: Area of Effect (AoE), Weapon Enhancer

Damage: Base: 25 HP, 50% AP. Shotgun base: 25 HP, 200% AP.

Effect: Trigger a spray of projectiles on the last hit of each normal attack combo.

Location: Products

BOOST OF VICTORY

Description: After defeating an enemy, your knight heals and grows in size! After fifteen seconds, your knight returns to normal size.

Category: Offensive

Element: Armor

Type: Area of Effect (AoE), Weapon Enhancer

Damage: Base: 25 HP, 40% AP (can stack damage).

Effect: Destroying an enemy gives a stack. Knight gets 20% bigger on each stack. Heals for 3% max HP when you get a stack.

Location: TV Show

BOWLING CYCLONE

Description: Launch a powerful whirling tornado, complete with flying bowling balls, toward your enemies! This Power hits them hard and stuns them.

Category: Offensive

Element: Air

Type: Area of Effect (AoE), Weapon Enhancer

Damage: Tornado Base: 50 HP, DoT 150% AP/second. Ball Base: 50 HP, 400% AP.

Effect: Throws a ball every second.

Location: TV Show

BOWMASTER

Description: An arrow-shooting Squirebot goes wild on your enemies.

Category: Offensive

Element: Weapon

Type: Area of Effect (AoE), Weapon Enhancer

Damage: Base: 50 HP, 400% AP.

Effect: Summon a Bowmaster Squirebot. The Bowmaster can be attacked if he is the closest target for enemies.

Location: Products

BRACER OF STRENGTH

Description: Your knight can equip these bracers to experience a surge in strength.

Category: Supportive

Element: Armor

Type: Self

Damage: Base: 25 HP, 110% AP.

Effect: Knock back.

Location: In-store

BRAIN FREEZE

Description: Freeze your enemies' brains, preventing them from using their special abilities and powers.

Category: Offensive

Element: Ice

Type: Area of Effect (AoE), Weapon Enhancer

Damage: Base: 25 HP.

Effect: Freezes and confuses all enemies on-screen. Damage dealt to frozen enemies is increased by 15%.

Location: LEGOLAND, In-store

BROCCOLI TORNADO

Description: Your knight summons a tornado that tosses the baddies around. This tornado also drops delicious broccoli, which your knight can eat to restore health.

Category: Offensive

Element: Air

Type: Area of Effect (AoE), Weapon Enhancer

Damage: Base DoT: 50 HP, 100% AP/second.

Effect: Heal 2% of max health for each broccoli eaten.

Location: LEGOLAND, In-store

BROKEN HEART

Description: A giant heart drops down on the battlefield. Each time your knight hits it, red hearts drop out. You can pick these up for extra health!

Category: Offensive

Element: Magic

Type: Area of Effect (AoE), Weapon Enhancer

Damage: Base: 50 HP, 200% AP.

Effect: Spawns five small hearts, each healing 2% of your knight's max HP.

Location: Merlok 2.0 App

BROOM OF DOOM

Description: Sweep your enemies off their feet—literally—with this massive and threatening broom.

Category: Offensive

Element: Air

Type: Area of Effect (AoE), Weapon Enhancer

Damage: Base: 50 HP, 300% AP per hit.

Effect: N/A

Location: LEGO.COM, In-store

BUBBLE GUM MISFIRE

Description: Create a big bubble o' gum around your knight. Enemies who try to enter the sticky sphere will be slowed down, and projectiles will be reflected back at the enemy.

Category: Defensive

Element: Armor

Type: Self

Damage: N/A

Effect: Slows enemy movement and attacks by 20%. Reflects projectiles.

Location: LEGO Club Magazine, In-store

BULL RACE

Description: A stampeding horde of bulls races across the battlefield, damaging and stunning trampled enemies.

Category: Offensive

Element: Animal

Type: Area of Effect (AoE), Weapon Enhancer

Damage: Base: 100 HP, 400% AP.

Effect: Knock upward.

Location: Products

BULLDOZER

Description: A bulldozer rumbles across the battlefield, smashing enemies as it goes.

Category: Offensive

Element: Armor

Type: Area of Effect (AoE), Weapon Enhancer

Damage: Base: 100 HP, 750% AP to all enemies.

Effect: Push all enemies to the left or right side of the screen.

Location: Products

BULLFROG SUPERBOUND

Description: A giant frog appears and stomps several times on the bad guys.

Category: Offensive

Element: Animal

Type: Area of Effect (AoE), Weapon Enhancer

Damage: Base: 50 HP, 250% AP.

Effect: Every two seconds, a frog jumps out and lands next to your knight.

Location: Extended line, In-store

BURNT HOT DOG

Description: Have yourself a baddie BBQ! If they're on the grill long enough, they turn into hot dogs, which you can eat to regain health.

Category: Offensive

Element: Food

Type: Area of Effect (AoE), Weapon Enhancer

Damage: Base DoT: 50 HP, 150% AP/second.

Effect: Enemies take fire damage. Destroying a burning enemy spawns a hot dog. Eating a hot dog heals your knight for 8% of their max HP.

Location: Products

CANDY FLOSS

Description: Strike your enemies with candy floss, then eat it! You'll drain health from your enemies.

Category: Offensive

Element: Food

Type: Area of Effect (AoE), Weapon Enhancer

Damage: Base: 25 HP, 200% AP for each enemy affected.

Effect: Heals your knight for 20% of the damage done.

Location: In-store

CARROT MISSILE

Description: Carrots rain down from the sky on your foes! When they land, they burrow into the ground and become carrot bombs.

Category: Offensive

Element: Food

Type: Area of Effect (AoE), Weapon Enhancer

Damage: Base: 25 HP, 100% AP. Explosion Base: 50 HP, 300% AP.

Effect: Each carrot explosion heals your knight for 3% of their max HP.

Location: LEGOLAND

CENTAUR CHARGE

Description: A mighty centaur barrels toward your enemies, knocking them back and damaging them.

Category: Offensive

Element: Monster

Type: Area of Effect (AoE), Weapon Enhancer

Damage: Base: 100 HP, 400% AP.

Effect: Knock back.

Location: Products

CENTIPEDE

Description: Your enemies will follow your knight around in a silly conga line. The more enemies, the greater damage they will take when the party is over!

Category: Offensive

Element: Insect

Type: Area of Effect (AoE), Weapon Enhancer

Damage: Base: 50 HP, 400% AP for each enemy affected.

Effect: N/A

Location: In-store

"You set 'em up, I'll knock 'em down!"
—Clay

CHAMPION OF CHIVALRY

Description: Your knight turns into a champion! Your chances of landing a critical strike and the critical strike damage are increased.

Category: Offensive

Element: Weapon

Type: Area of Effect (AoE), Weapon Enhancer

Damage: Base: 50 HP.

Effect: Increase critical strike chance by 15% and critical strike damage by 50%.

Location: LEGO.COM, In-store

CHARGING ATTACK

Description: Charge more powerfully into your enemies.

Category: Offensive

Element: Armor

Type: Self

Damage: N/A

Effect: All regular attacks become charged attacks that deal twice the damage for a short duration.

Location: Products

CHICKEN POWER

Description: Invoke the Power of the Chicken! Call a hail of eggs down on your enemies and damage them all.

Category: Offensive

Element: Bird

Type: Summoning

Damage: Base: 50 HP, 125% AP per egg.

Effect: Slow movement and attack by 25%.

Location: Products

CHILI CON CARNE

Description: Unleash fiery breath on your foes! Beware—it's even hotter than Gobbleton Rambley's hottest ever chili!

Category: Offensive

Element: Food

Type: Area of Effect (AoE), Weapon Enhancer

Damage: Base Pepper: 50 HP, 300% AP. AoE Base: 25 HP, 200% AP.

Effect: Burning.

Location: Merlok 2.0 App, In-store

CHIMERA OF COURTESY

Description: Take on some of the mighty Chimera's powers. Adds poison damage to your weapon and regenerates health and raises defense for a short time.

Category: Offensive

Element: Monster

Type: Area of Effect (AoE), Weapon Enhancer

Damage: Base: 25 HP, 25% poison damage on basic attacks.

Effect: Heals your knight for 15% of their max health. Increases defense by 15%.

Location: TV Show

CHROME BELL

Description: Three chrome bells drop on the battlefield. You can hit them all to create a tone that damages all opponents or ring one for AoE damage.

Category: Offensive

Element: Sound

Type: Area of Effect (AoE), Weapon Enhancer

Damage: 100, 1 Bell Damage: 500% AP, 2 Bells Damage: 1000% AP, 3 Bells Damage: 1500% AP.

Effect: Knock back on attacks.

Location: Extended line

CLAPPERCLAW

Description: Summon the might of the red dragon and deal massive damage to a single enemy with its five-claw attack.

Category: Offensive

Element: Monster

Type: Automatic

Damage: Base: 50 HP, 200% AP (x10).

Effect: N/A

Location: Products, LEGO.COM

CLEANSING RAIN

Description: Surround your knight with a healing dome and damage your enemies with harsh rain!

Category: Offensive

Element: Water

Type: Area of Effect (AoE), Weapon Enhancer

Damage: Base Rain DoT: 25 HP/second, 100% AP.

Effect: Prevent enemies from entering the dome. Heal your knight for 2% of their max HP.

Location: In-store

CLONING

Description: Multiple copies of your knight appear and function as decoys that confuse your enemies.

Category: Defensive

Element: Armor

Type: Summoning

Damage: N/A

Effect: Create three copies of your knight that last until they are hit three times.

Location: Products, LEGO.COM

CLOVER OF MISFORTUNE

Description: Your knight cannot deal or receive damage, but your skills charge faster while attacking.

Category: Offensive

Element: Plant

Type: Area of Effect (AoE), Weapon Enhancer

Damage: N/A

Effect: Charge attacks 100% faster.

Location: In-store, Products

COBRA BACKSTAB

Description: Time slows down and allows your knight to attack enemies multiple times.

Category: Offensive

Element: Animal

Type: Area of Effect (AoE), Weapon Enhancer

Damage: Base: 100 HP, 1200% AP on each enemy.

Effect: N/A

Location: In-store

COMMANDING SHOUT

Description: Emit a commanding shout that paralyzes enemies nearby.

Category: Supportive

Element: Armor

Type: Cone

Damage: N/A

Effect: Stun enemies. Heal your knight for 6% of their max HP when they shout.

Location: Products

COOL CREATION

Description: A pyramid appears—but it's upside down! Knock it over to make it explode and cause damage.

Category: Offensive

Element: Magic

Type: Area of Effect (AoE), Weapon Enhancer

Damage: Base: 100 HP, 1000% AP.

Effect: N/A

Location: LEGO Club Magazine, Products

COOL MOVES

Description: Your knight can freeze enemies in their tracks.

Category: Offensive

Element: Ice

Type: Area of Effect (AoE), Weapon Enhancer

Damage: Frost Nova Base: 50 HP, 250% AP. Frost Explosion Base: 25 HP, 150% AP.

Effect: Freeze enemies.

Location: In-store

CRIMSON BAT

Description: Bats surround your knight and fly toward the enemy, sucking their life away and giving it back to your knight.

Category: Offensive

Element: Animal

Type: Area of Effect (AoE), Weapon Enhancer

Damage: Base: 75 HP, 150% AP/second.

Effect: Gain 20% of damage done in HP.

Location: Products

CROC TEARS

Description: Creates a giant pool of water. When your enemies walk over it, a huge crocodile emerges to snap at them, damaging and paralyzing them.

Category: Offensive

Element: Animal

Type: Area of Effect (AoE), Weapon Enhancer

Damage: Base: 75 HP, 625% AP.

Effect: Paralyze enemies.

Location: Products, LEGO.COM

CRYSTAL BALLS

Description: Three crystal balls appear and hypnotize your enemies—until they explode and cause damage!

Category: Offensive

Element: Magic

Type: Area of Effect (AoE), Weapon Enhancer

Damage: Base: 50 HP, 400% AP.

Effect: Blind enemies.

Location: TV Show

"So shiny—I've gotta have 'em!"

—Lance

CYCLONIC STRIKE

Description: A massive fist whirls around your knight, damaging enemies and knocking them into the air.

Category: Offensive

Element: Air

Type: Area of Effect (AoE), Weapon Enhancer

Damage: Base: 50 HP, 350% AP.

Effect: Knock upward.

Location: LEGO.COM, In-store

DARING DELIVERANCE

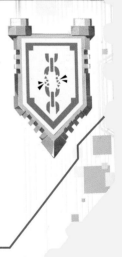

Description: Remove and prevent any negative effects on your knight.

Category: Supportive

Element: Magic

Type: Self

Damage: N/A

Effect: Removes any negative effects. Your knight is immune to them for five seconds.

Location: TV Show, In-store

DARK DROP

Description: Squirt a trail of ink that damages and blinds your enemy.

Category: Offensive

Element: Animal

Type: Area of Effect (AoE), Weapon Enhancer

Damage: Base DoT: 25 HP, 100% AP/second.

Effect: Blind and confuse your enemies.

Location: Books, Products

DAZZLING HERO

Description: Invigorate your knight by bathing them in yellow energy.

Category: Supportive

Element: Armor

Type: Self

Damage: Varies

Effect: All attacks are critical hits.

Location: LEGO.COM, In-store

DAZZLING LURE

Description: A light probe pops out of the ground, luring enemies to it. After five seconds, a giant fish jaw snaps your enemies and damages them.

Category: Offensive

Element: Animal

Type: Area of Effect (AoE), Weapon Enhancer

Damage: Base: 100 HP, 875% AP.

Effect: Draw all enemies toward the probe.

Location: Extended line, In-store

DEPTH CHARGE

Description: Your knight burrows underground. The first enemy your knight encounters while burrowing pops the knight back out of the ground, damaging your enemy and pushing them back.

Category: Offensive

Element: Earth

Type: Area of Effect (AoE), Weapon Enhancer

Damage: Base: 100 HP, 1000% AP.

Effect: Knock back. Your knight moves 30% slower while underground.

Location: In-store

DIAMOND SPEAR

Description: Pick a target and launch a sparkly spear toward them.

Category: Offensive

Element: Weapon

Type: Area of Effect (AoE), Weapon Enhancer

Damage: Base: 50 HP, 250% AP.

Effect: Return 20% of damage dealt as health back to your knight.

Location: Products

DISCO FRENZY

Description: Three disco balls fall from the sky, exploding when they hit the ground. Three balls of light are created that spread in all directions.

Category: Offensive

Element: Light

Type: Area of Effect (AoE), Weapon Enhancer

Damage: Base: 100 HP, 200% AP for each disco ball.

Effect: Confuse nearby enemies.

Location: Books, In-store

DOWNSIZER

Description: Shrink all enemies by 50% and cause more damage! Careful, they're so small there's a chance you can miss them.

Category: Offensive

Element: Armor

Type: Area of Effect (AoE), Weapon Enhancer

Damage: Base: 25 HP.

Effect: Inflict 70% greater damage on shrunken enemies.

Location: Products, LEGO Club magazine

DRAGON OF JUSTICE

Description: Invoke the raging power of the dragon to create an offensive aura around your knight.

Category: Offensive

Element: Dragon

Type: Area of Effect (AoE), Weapon Enhancer

Damage: Base: 75 HP.

Effect: 200% of the damage received is redirected to your enemy.

Location: TV Show, LEGO.COM

DRAINING SCARF

Description: Entangle up to six enemies with scarves that look great but drain them of their health.

Category: Offensive

Element: Armor

Type: Area of Effect (AoE), Weapon Enhancer

Damage: Base: 75 HP, 75% AP/second.

Effect: 20% of damage done is returned to your knight as health.

Location: Products

DROP THE BEAT

Description: Blast your opponents with a cone of musical energy.

Category: Offensive

Element: Sound

Type: Area of Effect (AoE), Weapon Enhancer

Damage: Base: 25 HP, 125% AP.

Effect: N/A

Location: Products

DYNAMIGHTY

Description: Beware of falling dynamite! Once it hits the ground and explodes, five smaller sticks of dynamite appear.

Category: Offensive

Element: Explosion

Type: Area of Effect (AoE)

Damage: Base: 100 HP. Large stick: 500% AP. Smaller sticks: 200 AP.

Effect: N/A

Location: Products

EARTHQUAKE

Description: The battlefield is split in two by a giant crack. You can isolate enemies or even get them to fall into the crack.

Category: Offensive

Element: Earth

Type: Area of Effect (AoE), Weapon Enhancer

Damage: N/A

Effect: Destroy all non-elite, non-boss monsters standing on the crack. Enemies cannot cross the crack.

Location: LEGO Club Magazine

EGG OF DOOM

Description: A chicken runs amok on the battlefield and damages all enemies. First enemy to touch the chicken starts a five-second countdown to chicken explosion!

Category: Offensive

Element: Monster

Type: Area of Effect (AoE), Weapon Enhancer

Damage: Base: 100 HP, 1250% AP.

Effect: Aggravates all enemies.

Location: In-store, LEGO.COM

END OF TIME

Description: Each hit reduces the cooldown of skills by three (instead of one).

Category: Offensive

Element: Earth

Type: Area of Effect (AoE), Weapon Enhancer

Damage: N/A

Effect: Skill refresh rates are increased by 400% when using normal attacks.

Location: Extended line, LEGO.COM

"It's TIME we won this fight! Get it? Time?"

—Merlok 2.0

FALLEN HERO

Description: Brings your knight exploding back to life!

Category: Offensive

Element: Weapon

Type: Area of Effect (AoE), Weapon Enhancer

Damage: Base: 100 HP, 1000% AP.

Effect: If your knight has fallen, they return to life with 25% of their health.

Location: TV Show

FIRE TORNADO

Description: Summon a fiery tornado that moves toward enemies.

Category: Offensive

Element: Air

Type: Area of Effect (AoE), Summoning

Damage: Base DoT: 50 HP, 200% AP/second.

Effect: N/A

Location: Products

FIREFLIES

Description: Fireflies look pretty—until they EXPLODE on your enemies, that is!

Category: Offensive

Element: Fire

Type: Area of Effect (AoE), Weapon Enhancer

Damage: Base: 100 HP, Five hits—200-250-300-350-400% AP.

Effect: N/A

Location: LEGO.COM, In-store

FIST SMASH

Description: Five giant fists fall from the sky and pound enemies.

Category: Offensive

Element: Armor

Type: Area of Effect (frontal)

Damage: Base: 100 HP, 275% AP (x4). Shock wave: 125% (x4).

Effect: N/A

Location: Products

FLAME WRECK

Description: Grants your knight a weapon of FIRE!

Category: Supportive

Element: Weapon

Type: Self, Weapon Enhancer

Damage: Base: 25 HP.

Effect: Adds 50% of total weapon damage to each strike.

Location: Products

FLASH CANNON

Description: Emit a beam of light from your shield to blind and destroy enemies.

Category: Offensive

Element: Weapon

Type: Area of Effect (AoE), Weapon Enhancer

Damage: Base: 75 HP, 300% AP.

Effect: Blinds and confuses enemies.

Location: Products

FLIGHT OF THE PHOENIX

Description: Your knight disappears in a puff of smoke, leaving a pool of burning flames behind and reappears in a random location.

Category: Defensive

Element: Bird

Type: Area of Effect (around), Movement

Damage: Base: 50 HP and 200% AP/second.

Effect: N/A

Location: TV Show, In-store

FORCE FIELD

Description: Your knight invokes a protective shield that can withstand any attack. The shield becomes more transparent with each hit (100%, 66%, 33%).

Category: Defensive

Element: Armor

Type: Self

Damage: N/A

Effect: The next five attacks to hit your knight are reduced to 0 damage and conditions are nullified as well.

Location: Products

FORCE OF NATURE

Description: Summon vines from the ground that immobilize and damage foes.

Category: Offensive

Element: Plant

Type: Area of Effect (around)

Damage: Base DoT: 50 HP and 100% AP/second.

Effect: Enemies are immobilized.

Location: LEGO.COM, In-store

FORMATION OF FORTITUDE

Description: Creates four copies of your knight that will follow and copy you exactly. They form a square around your knight.

Category: Offensive

Element: Magic

Type: Area of Effect (AoE), Weapon Enhancer

Damage: Base: 50 HP. Copy damage: 25% of your knight's damage.

Effect: N/A

Location: LEGO.COM

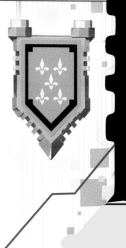

FOUL STEAM

Description: A big piece of cheese drops on the ground. When your knight eats it, a stinking cloud trail will follow where they walk. Enemies caught in the cloud take damage.

Category: Offensive

Element: Food

Type: Area of Effect (AoE), Weapon Enhancer

Damage: Base DoT: 50 HP and 125% AP/second within the cloud.

Effect: 20% of max HP restored.

Location: Products, In-store

FUNKY FUNGUS

Description: A small fungus pops up from the ground and begins singing a funky song. Nearby enemies are confused by the song and temporarily immobilized.

Category: Offensive

Element: Plant

Type: Area of Effect (AoE), Weapon Enhancer

Damage: N/A

Effect: Confuse nearby enemies.

Location: LEGO Club Magazine, LEGO.COM

GAMMA RAYS

Description: A massive laser erupts from your knight's shield. Enemies take damage and are blinded!

Category: Offensive

Element: Light

Type: Area of Effect (AoE), Weapon Enhancer

Damage: Base: 50 HP and 175% AP/second.

Effect: Blinds enemies.

Location: Products

GAUNTLET OF TRUTH

Description: Makes enemies more vulnerable to attacks.

Category: Offensive

Element: Armor

Type: Area of Effect (AoE), Weapon Enhancer

Damage: Base: 50 HP.

Effect: Adds vulnerability to all enemies, who receive 70% more damage.

Location: TV Show

GAZE OF THE GORGON

Description: Turn your enemies to stone with a deadly gaze.

Category: Offensive

Element: Monster

Type: Area of Effect (AoE), Weapon Enhancer

Damage: N/A

Effect: Petrify enemies, who still take damage normally.

Location: In-store, Products

"Very dangerous—
don't look at the
eyes!"

—CLAY

GIANT GROWTH

Description: Your knight becomes huge with incredible strength, but is clumsier than usual.

Category: Supportive

Element: Armor

Type: Self

Damage: Base: 25 HP.

Effect: Defense, Damage, and Speed increased by 50%.

Location: Products

GIGGLING ULTRA ARMOR

Description: Three feathers appear around your knight and act as a shield. Each time the knight is hit, a feather disappears and the enemy becomes confused.

Category: Defensive
Element: Bird
Type: Self
Damage: N/A
Effect: Confuses enemies.
Location: LEGO.COM, TV show

GLOBE OF LIGHT

Description: Your knight's shield sends out a globe of light in front of them, damaging all enemies. If the globe hits a knight, it is absorbed by the knight, improving their defense.

Category: Offensive, Defensive
Element: Light
Type: Area of Effect (AoE), Weapon Enhancer
Damage: Base DoT: 25 HP, 50% AP/second.
Effect: Recover 2% of max HP.
Location: LEGO.COM, Products

GLOBLIN ATTACK

Description: Your knight summons Globlins to attack enemies.
Category: Offensive
Element: Monster
Type: Summoning
Damage: Base: 50 HP.
Effect: Summon 1-3 Globlins (random). They are the same level as your knight.
Location: Products, In-store

GLORY OF KNIGHTON

Description: Marks your enemies with the king's crown.
Category: Offensive
Element: Animal
Type: Area of Effect (AoE), Weapon Enhancer
Damage: N/A
Effect: All enemies drop 200% more Memory Bits when defeated. Enemies have a 33% greater chance to drop Memory Bits.
Location: TV Show, Products

GOLDEN TOUCH

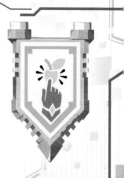

Description: Change a petrified enemy into Memory Bits.

Category: Offensive

Element: Food

Type: Area of Effect (AoE), Weapon Enhancer

Damage: N/A

Effect: Normal attacks have 25% chance to drop Memory Bits.

Location: In-store, Extended line

GOO GEYSER

Description: A Goo Geyser rockets up through the earth, flinging your enemies high in the air, then poisoning and slowing them as they land.

Category: Offensive

Element: Poison

Type: Area of Effect (AoE), Weapon Enhancer

Damage: Base: 75 HP, 900% AP (on landing).

Effect: Knock upward and slow movement by 30%.

Location: LEGOLAND, LEGO Club Magazine

GOOSE BUMPS

Description: A flock of geese frantically fly into your enemies, stunning them.

Category: Offensive

Element: Bird

Type: Area of Effect (all), Weapon Enhancer

Damage: Base: 75 HP, 400% AP.

Effect: Flatten and stun enemies.

Location: Products

GORILLA ROAR

Description: Your knight performs a huge *ROAR* and stuns all enemies!

Category: Offensive

Element: Animal

Type: Area of Effect (all), Weapon Enhancer

Damage: N/A

Effect: Afflict enemies with Fear. All frightened enemies take 100% more damage.

Location: Products

GRASSHOPPER

Description: Your knight can jump anywhere on-screen with great force, smashing all enemies on the ground.

Category: Offensive

Element: Insect

Type: Area of Effect (all), Weapon Enhancer

Damage: Base: 100 HP, 250% AP.

Effect: Knocks enemies back.

Location: In-store

GREATEST HITS

Description: Mimic the last Power your knight used.

Category: Offensive

Element: Sound

Type: Area of Effect (AoE), Weapon Enhancer

Damage: N/A

Effect: Mimic last Power used. If this is the first power your knight is using in the fight, one of the two other Powers will be selected randomly.

Location: Books, LEGOLAND

GRIFFIN OF GRACIOUSNESS

Description: The power of the mighty griffin increases your knight's defense and movement speed.

Category: Defensive

Element: Monster

Type: Self

Damage: N/A

Effect: Increases defense and movement speed by 25%.

Location: TV Show, Products

GROUND POUND

Description: SLAM your weapon into the ground, creating a powerful shock wave that stuns and damages all enemies.

Category: Offensive

Element: Earth

Type: Area of Effect (AoE), Weapon Enhancer

Damage: Base: 75 HP, 250% AP.

Effect: Stun your enemies.

Location: Products

GUARD DOG

Description: A dog house appears and when your enemies get too close, a fierce dog starts barking! Your enemies will flee in fear.

Category: Offensive

Element: Animal

Type: Area of Effect (all), Weapon Enhancer

Damage: Base: 50 HP, 200% AP.

Effect: N/A

Location: Extended line

HAIL TO THE JESTER

Description: Enemies are lured to a jack-in-the-box, which explodes in a shower of sparkles. All enemies are stunned briefly.

Category: Offensive

Element: Monster

Type: Area of Effect (AoE), Weapon Enhancer

Damage: N/A

Effect: Lure enemies for two seconds; glittering explosion stuns enemies for three seconds.

Location: TV Show, In-store

HAMMER SLAM

Description: Your knight creates a digital hammer that attacks nearby enemies.

Category: Offensive

Element: Weapon

Type: Summoning

Damage: Base: 50 HP, 250% AP.

Effect: N/A

Location: LEGO.COM, In-store

> *"Stop! I believe it's time to use the hammer."*
> —AVA

HAUNTED ARMOR

Description: Any time your knight takes damage, a ghastly ghost bursts forth from their armor to haunt your enemy and strike fear into them!

Category: Offensive

Element: Monster

Type: Area of Effect (AoE), Weapon Enhancer

Damage: Base DoT: 25 HP, 150% AP/second.

Effect: Inflict fear on your enemies.

Location: Products

HAWK HOLLER

Description: Your knight's shield emits a sonic shriek with the power of a hawk, paralyzing nearby enemies.
Category: Supportive
Element: Bird
Type: Cone
Damage: N/A
Effect: Paralyze
Location: Products, TV show

HONEY BEES

Description: BEEEEEEES! Bees swarm your enemies and attack!
Category: Offensive
Element: Insect
Type: Area of Effect (AoE), Weapon Enhancer
Damage: Base: 25 HP, 150% AP.
Effect: Send 2 wasps every second at the enemy closest to the hive. Slow movement speed by 25%.
Location: Products

HORNBLOWER

Description: Toot on a massive horn to sweep your enemies away in a shock wave!

Category: Offensive

Element: Sound

Type: Area of Effect (AoE), Weapon Enhancer

Damage: N/A

Effect: Increase your knight's movement speed by 25%. Inflict fear on all enemies.

Location: Products

HOWBLITZER

Description: Squirebot paparazzi follow your knight around and take pictures of them—fame has a price! The camera's bright flash blinds your enemies.

Category: Offensive

Element: Light

Type: Area of Effect (AoE), Weapon Enhancer

Damage: N/A

Effect: Blind your enemies.

Location: In-store

HYDRA'S BLAST

Description: Toast your enemies with a blast from this fearsome Hydra.

Category: Offensive

Element: Dragon

Type: Area of Effect (AoE), Weapon Enhancer

Damage: Base: 50 HP and 150% AP/beam.

Effect: N/A

Location: TV show

HYPER KICK

Description: Knock your enemies flying into the air with a fierce kick! Enemies take damage when they land.

Category: Offensive

Element: Armor

Type: Area of Effect (AoE), Weapon Enhancer

Damage: Base: 25 HP, 50% AP on normal attacks. 400% AP on landing.

Effect: Knock upward.

Location: In-store, Products

ICE BURST

Description: Giant ice crystals smash into your opponents, dealing moderate damage. If your enemy has been slowed, they freeze and take damage again.

Category: Offensive

Element: Ice

Type: Area of Effect (AoE), Weapon Enhancer

Damage: Base: 75 HP, 500% AP explosion damage.

Effect: Freeze your enemies.

Location: In-store

ICE CREAM

Description: Your knight's main weapon is replaced by ice cream! Enemies take normal damage but have a greater chance of being frozen.

Category: Offensive

Element: Food

Type: Area of Effect (AoE), Weapon Enhancer

Damage: Base: 50 HP, 150% AP on frozen enemy.

Effect: Enemies have a 15% chance of being frozen when attacked.

Location: Products

ICE DRAGON

Description: Leave a trail of ice on the ground to slow down your enemies. Spikes of ice will shoot up from the ground, damaging all who are near.

Category: Supportive

Element: Dragon

Type: Area of Effect (AoE), Weapon Enhancer

Damage: Base: 100 HP, 450% AP.

Effect: Attack and movement slowed by 25%.

Location: Products

ICE RAIN

Description: Ice spikes rain down from the sky every half second on random enemies.

Category: Offensive

Element: Ice

Type: Area of Effect (AoE), Weapon Enhancer

Damage: Base DoT: 50 HP, 200% AP per spike.

Effect: 100% chance to freeze your enemies when hit.

Location: Products

INCINERATE

Description: Flaming fireballs launch from your shield and land on random enemies every half second.

Category: Offensive

Element: Fire

Type: Area of Effect (around)

Damage: Base: 50 HP, 175% AP per fireball

Effect: N/A

Location: Products

INVERTED CHARGE

Description: Your knight builds up a huge charge. The longer you can avoid getting hit by an enemy, the greater the attack will be.

Category: Offensive

Element: Magic

Type: Area of Effect (AoE), Weapon Enhancer

Damage: Base: 25–50 HP, 1000–2000% AP depending on energy charged.

Effect: Power increases 10% every second. Every time your knight takes damage, your Power decreases by 10%.

Location: In-store

IRON DRAGON

Description: Put the fear of the dragon into your enemies!

Category: Offensive

Element: Dragon

Type: Area of Effect (AoE), Weapon Enhancer

Damage: Base: 50 HP, 250% AP.

Effect: Knock back and stun your enemies.

Location: Products

IRON HAIR

Description: Your knight is covered in spiky metallic hair. Enemies who strike your knight will take damage.

Category: Offensive

Element: Magic

Type: Supportive, Defensive

Damage: Base: 50 HP.

Effect: Increase knight's defense by 25%. Inflict 150% of damage done by your enemies back to them.

Location: In-store

JUMPERMAN

Description: A bomb appears at your knight's feet and launches them into the air. Aim your knight at a target on the ground and they will land and deal massive damage.

Category: Offensive

Element: Explosion

Type: Area of Effect (AoE), Weapon Enhancer

Damage: Base: 50 HP, 450% AP. Landing damage: 50 HP, 550% AP.

Effect: Bomb explosions knock back your enemies.

Location: Products

"Bomb-tastic!"
—MACY

JUNGLE DRAGON

Description: Leave a trail of poisonous liquid on the ground, damaging all enemies who walk on it. If your enemy walks on the poison three times, vines emerge from it to immobilize your enemy.

Category: Offensive

Element: Dragon

Type: Trail

Damage: Base: 50 HP, 100% AP/second.

Effect: Immobilize enemies for five seconds.

Location: Products

LAVA DRAGON

Description: Your knight leaves a trail of fire on the ground, toasting your enemies as they walk through it. Upon completion, the flames will explode in a fiery conflagration, damaging all enemies.

Category: Offensive

Element: Dragon

Type: Area of Effect (AoE), Trail

Damage: Base: 100 HP, 100% AP/second. DoT: 25 HP. Fire Nova: 450% AP.

Effect: Burns your enemies over time.

Location: Products

LION OF BRAVERY

Description: Invoke the power of a mighty lion to improve your attack!

Category: Offensive

Element: Animal

Type: Area of Effect (AoE), Weapon Enhancer

Damage: Base: 50 HP.

Effect: Improve your knight's damage by 50% and critical chance by 15%.

Location: TV Show, In-store

LOADMASTER

Description: A big, slow Squirebot appears, jumping high in the air and smashing down on your enemies.

Category: Offensive

Element: Air

Type: Area of Effect, Weapon Enhancer

Damage: Base: 50 HP, 300% AP.

Effect: Flatten and stun your enemies.

Location: Products

LOCKSMITH

Description: A large treasure chest appears on the battlefield, attracting monsters that attempt to smash it open. After ten seconds, it opens automatically and explodes!

Category: Offensive

Element: Weapon

Type: Area of Effect, Weapon Enhancer

Damage: Base: 50 HP, 400% AP.

Effect: Lure all enemies toward the chest.

Location: LEGO Club Magazine

LONG GONG

Description: A large gong appears in a random location. When struck, it makes an ear-splitting noise.

Category: Offensive

Element: Sound

Type: Area of Effect, Weapon Enhancer

Damage: Base: 50 HP, 500% AP.

Effect: Stun your enemies.

Location: Merlok 2.0 App, LEGO.COM

LORD HELMET

Description: Mind control your enemies so they fight for you!

Category: Offensive

Element: Magic

Type: Area of Effect, Weapon Enhancer

Damage: Varies.

Effect: The first enemy your knight hits now fights for you. The converted enemy taunts other nearby enemies, forcing them to aim at him.

Location: In-store

LUCKY BREAK

Description: A big horseshoe appears above your knight's head and sucks more Memory Bits out of your enemies.

Category: Offensive

Element: Magic

Type: Area of Effect (all), Weapon Enhancer

Damage: N/A

Effect: All enemies drop 50% more Memory Bits when defeated. Enemies have 100% greater chance of dropping Memory Bits.

Location: TV Show

MACE RAIN

Description: Giant maces fall from the sky and whack random nearby enemies, damaging and stunning them.

Category: Offensive

Element: Weapon

Type: Area of Effect (around)

Damage: Base DoT: 50 HP, 200% AP per mace (x5).

Effect: Stun your enemies.

Location: Products

MAGIC ANTI-EVIL ULTRA ARMOR UPGRADE

Description: Creates an aura of pure energy that increases your knight's armor. Enemies who stand close to your knight take damage over time.

Category: Defensive

Element: Fire

Type: Self

Damage: Base DoT: 50 HP, 100% AP.

Effect: Increase your knight's defense by 20%.

Location: TV Show, LEGO.COM

MAGIC BLAST

Description: Let loose a magical explosion on the baddies! Every enemy your knight hits is affected, and so are the bad guys around them.

Category: Offensive

Element: Magic

Type: Area of Effect (all), Weapon Enhancer

Damage: Base: 50 HP, 500% AP.

Effect: N/A

Location: TV Show

MAGMA BURST

Description: A fiery eruption of magma appears on the battlefield, damaging all enemies in the vicinity.

Category: Defensive

Element: Fire

Type: Self

Damage: Base: 100 HP, 500% AP. DoT: 25 HP. Burn Damage: 100% AP/second.

Effect: Chance of burning. If enemy is burning, they receive a critical hit.

Location: In-store

MAGNETIZE

Description: A mystic energy draws all enemies together in the middle of the screen, where they take damage and are stunned.

Category: Supportive

Element: Air

Type: Area of Effect (all)

Damage: Base: 100 HP, 250% AP (+100 AP per enemy pulled).

Effect: Move enemies to center of the screen and stun them.

Location: Products

MAJESTY OF BENEVOLENCE

Description: Delicious chicken legs rain down on the battlefield and heal your knight.

Category: Supportive

Element: Armor

Type: AoE (all)

Damage: N/A

Effect: Three chicken legs drop which heal 15% of total health each.

Location: TV Show

MAMMOTH

Description: A huge mammoth stomps on the battlefield, squashing your enemies.

Category: Offensive

Element: Monster

Type: Area of Effect (all), Weapon Enhancer

Damage: Base: 100 HP, 500% AP.

Effect: Flatten and stun enemies.

Location: Products

MANIC PUMPKIN

Description: A pumpkin that looks strangely like a Globlin appears to challenge your enemies. Leaves health upon defeat.

Category: Defensive

Element: Food

Type: Self

Damage: N/A

Effect: Inflict fear on surrounding enemies. Pumpkin explodes into five smaller pumpkins that your knight can eat to regain health—3% max HP each.

Location: Products

MANOWAR

Description: Terrible tentacles appear over your enemies and lash them, dealing damage and paralyzing them.

Category: Offensive

Element: Animal

Type: Area of Effect (all), Weapon Enhancer

Damage: Base: 50 HP, 250% AP per strike.

Effect: Paralyze your enemies.

Location: In-store

"Harness the power of the kraken!"
—CLAY

MANTIS EMBRACE

Description: Your knight can slash and strike enemies with giant mantis arms.

Category: Defensive

Element: Insect

Type: Self

Damage: Base: 25 HP (x2), 50% AP (x2).

Effect: Your knight can't use charged attacks while this Power is active.

Location: In-store

MASSIVE FAJITAS

Description: The sky is raining delicious fajitas, which smash into your enemies. They leave behind a puddle of fajita juice on the ground, which slows any monster caught in it. Your knight will regain health by standing in the fajita juice!

Category: Offensive

Element: Food

Type: Area of Effect (all), Weapon Enhancer

Damage: Base: 25% HP DoT, 100% AP/second.

Effect: Summons six yummy fajitas that heal for 8% of max HP.

Location: TV Show

MAX POWER

Description: YOU HAVE THE POWER! Buffs up your attack to maximum damage.

Category: Defensive

Element: Magic

Type: Self

Damage: N/A

Effect: Maximum damage dealth by attack is increased by 150% (minimum damage remains unchanged).

Location: LEGO Club Magazine, TV Show

MECH MASTER

Description: Your knight summons a Squirebot to aid them in battle.

Category: Supportive

Element: Armor

Type: Summoning

Damage: Base: 50 HP; Squirebot stats: HP = 25% of knight's total HP, 250% of knight's attack, same move speed and critical hit rate.

Effect: Squirebot's health is 25% of the knight's total HP.

Location: Products, In-store

MECHANICAL GRIFFIN

Description: Summon a powerful griffin ally to aid your knight in battle.

Category: Defensive

Element: Monster

Type: Self

Damage: Base DoT: 50 HP, 200% AP per feather.

Effect: Stun your enemies.

Location: Products

METAL MINOTAUR

Description: Your knight wears a mighty metal Minotaur helmet, which enables them to perform a rushing strike attack at enemies.

Category: Offensive

Element: Animal

Type: Area of Effect (all), Weapon Enhancer

Damage: Base: 25 HP.

Effect: Defense increased by 25%, damage increased by 50%.

Location: Products

MIGHT OF THE MAGICIAN

Description: Launch a continuous beam of FIRE at your enemies.
Category: Offensive
Element: Magic
Type: Line (through)
Damage: Base DoT: 50 HP, 300% AP/second.
Effect: N/A
Location: TV Show, Products

MIGHTINESS

Description: Knights are invigorated by a luminous yellow energy that envelops them.
Category: Supportive
Element: Magic
Type: Self
Damage: Base: 25 HP.
Effect: Improves damage by 90%.
Location: Products

MIGHTY PEN

Description: Two large pens appear around your knight and move "write" around them. The pens will instantly destroy smaller minions and make larger enemies vulnerable.

Category: Offensive

Element: Bird

Type: Area of Effect (all)

Damage: N/A

Effect: Returns small minions to the Book of Monsters for an instant defeat; big enemies take 50% more damage.

Location: In-store

MINDBENDER

Description: Hypnotize and stun your enemies.

Category: Offensive

Element: Magic

Type: Area of Effect (all), Weapon Enhancer

Damage: N/A

Effect: Confuse your enemies and slow them by 25%. Confused enemies can't attack.

Location: Products

MINIFY SURPRISE

Description: Your knight shrinks by 50% and their defense increases.

Category: Defensive

Element: Armor

Type: Self

Damage: N/A

Effect: Movement speed is increased by 30%, defense is increased by 40%.

Location: Extended line, In-store

MIRROR ME

Description: A ghostly knight shape follows your knight around and does what you do! All enemies in range will be hit by your clone's attacks.

Category: Offensive

Element: Armor

Type: Area of Effect (all), Weapon Enhancer

Damage: N/A

Effect: Creates a copy of your knight.

Location: Products

MONSOON STORM

Description: Violent rain pours down from the sky and slows all enemies.

Category: Offensive

Element: Air

Type: Self

Damage: N/A

Effect: Heals your knight for 2% of their max HP every second. Slow all enemy attacks and movement by 25%.

Location: In-store, TV Show

MOTH SWARM

Description: A very large moth flies from one side of the screen to the other. All enemies on-screen become vulnerable to normal attacks.

Category: Offensive

Element: Insect

Type: Area of Effect (all), Weapon Enhancer

Damage: Base: 50 HP.

Effect: Enemies take 60% more damage from normal attacks.

Location: Books, In-store

MOUSETRAP

Description: Launches five mouse-traps to snag enemies and five hunks of cheese to replenish your knight's health.

Category: Offensive, Supportive

Element: Animal

Type: Area of Effect (all), Weapon Enhancer

Damage: Base: 100 HP, 350% AP (trap damage).

Effect: Cheese heals 2% of your knight's max HP.

Location: LEGOLAND, Products

NEEDLE STORM

Description: Three storms of needles damage any enemies close by and follow your knight everywhere.

Category: Defensive

Element: Air

Type: Self

Damage: Base: 25 HP, 100% AP per needle.

Effect: Enemies are slowed by 33%

Location: Extended line

NEXO BLADE

Description: Your knight's weapon is enchanted with NEXO energy and can trigger chain lightning strikes when hitting an enemy!

Category: Offensive

Element: Weapon

Type: Self

Damage: Base: 50 HP, Target #1 = 250% AP, Target #2 = 200% AP, Target #3 = 150% AP (hit up to three targets).

Effect: N/A

Location: In-store, Products

NIGHTMARE LULLABY

Description: Sing a super-creepy lullaby to your enemies and watch them flee before your horrible song ends!

Category: Defensive

Element: Sound

Type: Self

Damage: N/A

Effect: Inflict Fear on your enemies. Heal your knight for 10% of the damage dealt.

Location: In-store

NINJA STRIKE

Description: Spin in place and throw ninja shurikens in any direction for ten seconds.

Category: Offensive

Element: Weapon

Type: Area of Effect (all), Weapon Enhancer

Damage: Base: 50 HP, 150% AP.

Effect: Turn your enemies into bowling pins!

Location: Products

ORBITAL STRIKE

Description: Take out multiple enemies from orbit! It's the only way to be sure.

Category: Defensive

Element: Weapon

Type: Self

Damage: Base: 50 HP, 350% AP per beam.

Effect: N/A

Location: Products

ORDER OF THE KNIGHTS CODE

Description: Become as fast as Aaron, strong as Axl, healthy as Macy, and resistant as Lance. Stare piercingly like Clay.

Category: Defensive, Supportive

Element: Armor

Type: Self

Damage: Base: 50 HP.

Effect: Increase movement by 15%, damage and defense by 30%.

Location: TV Show

OUT OF SOAP

Description: A gross green cloud surrounds your knight, and your enemies flee before the terrible stench.

Category: Offensive (super offensive!)

Element: Poison

Type: AOE (all), Weapon Enhancer

Damage: Base DoT: 25 HP and 100% AP/second.

Effect: Inflict fear on your enemies.

Location: Products

PAPRIKA BOLT

Description: A massive missile strikes in an explosion of paprika. You were expecting something else? We ran out of coriander.

Category: Offensive

Element: Food

Type: Area of Effect (all), Weapon Enhancer

Damage: Base DoT: 50 HP and 100% AP/second.

Effect: N/A

Location: TV Show

PHOENIX BLAZE

Description: Your knight is imbued with the power of the Phoenix (so rad!).

Category: Defensive

Element: Weapon

Type: Self

Damage: Base DoT: 25 HP.

Effect: Inflicts +33% fire damage. Upon defeat, your knight comes back to life with 30% health.

Location: Products

PIE GUARD

Description: Your Squirebot lets loose, flinging pies at you and replenishing health at an alarming rate!

Category: Supportive

Element: Food

Type: Self

Damage: Base: 25 HP, 100% AP.

Effect: Throws one pie per second. Pie heals your knight for 4% of their max HP.

Location: Products

PINBALL MAGICIAN

Description: Send a big 'ol marble bouncing on top of your enemies.

Category: Offensive

Element: Magic

Type: Area of Effect (all), Weapon Enhancer

Damage: Base: 100 HP, 300% AP.

Effect: N/A

Location: LEGOLAND, Products

PIRANHA BITE

Description: Drop a trap that appears to be a pool of water but is really infested with chompy piranhas. Yikes!

Category: Offensive

Element: Animal

Type: Trap

Damage: Base DoT: 25 HP, 100% AP per piranha bite.

Effect: Paralyze your enemies, summon a pool with up to twenty piranhas.

Location: Books, LEGO.COM

POISON BURST

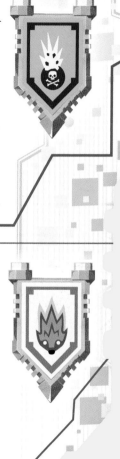

Description: Five projectiles spread out around your knight and then explode and release poison gas.

Category: Offensive

Element: Poison

Type: Area of Effect (all), Weapon Enhancer

Damage: Base: 100 HP, 500% AP explosion damage.

Effect: Slow movement and attacks by 20%.

Location: Merlok 2.0 App

PORCUPINE HUG

Description: Spikes grow from your knight and enemies stick to them. Damage is dealt for the duration of the Power.

Category: Offensive

Element: Animal

Type: Area of Effect (all), Weapon Enhancer

Damage: Base DoT: 25 HP, 125% AP/second.

Effect: Knight movement speed is reduced as enemies stick to your knight.

Location: In-store

POTENT PEPPERY POWER AXE

Description: Throw down red peppers and your enemies eat them, then take fire damage. Hot stuff!

Category: Offensive

Element: Food

Type: Area of Effect (all), Weapon Enhancer

Damage: Base DoT: 50 HP, 100% AP/second.

Effect: Fire damage.

Location: TV Show, LEGO.COM

POWDER KEG

Description: Destroy your enemies with a huge explosion!

Category: Offensive

Element: Explosion

Type: Area of Effect (all), Weapon Enhancer

Damage: Base: 100 HP, 700% AP.

Effect: N/A

Location: TV Show

"Here comes the BOOM!"
—LANCE

POWER GLUE

Description: Shoot a cone of Kragle glue at your enemies and freeze them for a REALLY long time!

Category: Offensive

Element: Water

Type: Area of Effect (all), Weapon Enhancer

Damage: N/A

Effect: Paralyze any enemy that moves over the glue.

Location: In-store

POWER OF UNITED KNIGHTS

Description: Assemble your fellow knights to assist you in the heat of battle.

Category: Offensive

Element: Armor

Type: Area of Effect (all), Weapon Enhancer

Damage: N/A

Effect: Summon a random knight.

Location: In-store

POWER PLANT

Description: Plant a hungry carnivorous plant on the ground to attack unsuspecting enemies.

Category: Offensive

Element: Plant

Type: Area of Effect (all), Weapon Enhancer

Damage: Base: 50 HP, 250% AP per plant bite.

Effect: Bites enemies every two seconds.

Location: In-store, Products

PRISM OF CLARITY

Description: A beam of light illuminates your knight and splits into four colorful rays that launch in front of them.

Category: Offensive

Element: Light

Type: Area of Effect (all), Weapon Enhancer

Damage: Base: 100 HP; Red beam = 375% AP fire, Blue beam = 375% AP ice, Yellow beam = 375% AP electricity, Green beam = 375% AP poison/acid.

Effect: N/A

Location: Products, LEGO.COM

PRUNE JUICE

Description: A prune a day keeps your enemies away!

Category: Offensive

Element: Food

Type: Area of Effect (all), Weapon Enhancer

Damage: Base DoT: 25 HP, 100% AP/second.

Effect: Taunt your enemies.

Location: Merlok 2.0 App

QUAKE BALL

Description: Spawn a huge soccer ball on the battlefield. Kick it at your enemies and watch them quake (literally!).

Category: Offensive

Element: Earth

Type: Area of Effect (all), Weapon Enhancer

Damage: Base: 100 HP, 300% AP.

Effect: N/A

Location: In-store, LEGO.COM

QUICKSAND

Description: Slow down your enemies with a quagmire of quicksand!

Category: Offensive

Element: Earth

Type: Area of Effect (all), Weapon Enhancer

Damage: N/A

Effect: Enemy movement speed and attack are slowed by 25%.

Location: LEGO.COM, LEGOLAND

RAGING RALLY

Description: Transform damage taken by your knight into healing instead!

Category: Defensive

Element: Animal

Type: Self

Damage: N/A

Effect: 66% of damage received is converted into healing.

Location: In-store, Products

RAPTOR BITE

Description: Four bear traps shaped like raptor heads appear around your knight and viciously snap at enemies who wander into them.

Category: Offensive

Element: Monster

Type: Area of Effect (all), Weapon Enhancer

Damage: Base: 100 HP, 500% AP/second (small AoE).

Effect: N/A

Location: In-store, LEGOLAND

RAT TIDE

Description: Launch three waves of rats at your enemies! *Eek, eeeeek!*

Category: Offensive

Element: Animal

Type: Area of Effect (all), Weapon Enhancer

Damage: Base: 75 HP, 25 HP DoT, 300% AP/wave; Poison damage 100% AP/second.

Effect: Poisons your enemies.

Location: LEGO Club Magazine, LEGO.COM

REMOTE CONTROL

Description: Drop a super-charged remote control on the battlefield that zaps your enemies with shocks of electricity. *Yow!*

Category: Offensive

Element: Electricity

Type: Area of Effect (all), Weapon Enhancer

Damage: Base: 50 HP, 250% AP/discharge.

Effect: N/A

Location: LEGO.COM

RIPPING THORNS

Description: Unleash a spiky, poisonous wave of thorns at your enemies.

Category: Offensive

Element: Plant

Type: Area of Effect (all), Weapon Enhancer

Damage: Base: 100 HP, 25 HP DoT, 625% AP; Poison damage 50% AP/second.

Effect: Poisons your enemies.

Location: Extended line, LEGO.COM

ROARING RIGHTEOUSNESS

Description: Your knight fiercely shouts and pushes enemies back, stunning them.

Category: Defensive

Element: Animal

Type: Area of Effect (all), Weapon Enhancer

Damage: N/A

Effect: Knock back and stun your enemies.

Location: LEGO.COM, Products

ROCK 'N' RUMBLE

Description: Throw falling rocks down on the baddies! Take cover!

Category: Offensive

Element: Earth

Type: Area of Effect (all), Weapon Enhancer

Damage: Base: 40 HP, 300% AP.

Effect: N/A

Location: TV Show

ROCK RIPPER

Description: Send three circular saws ripping through the ground (and your enemies).

Category: Offensive

Element: Earth

Type: Area of Effect (all), Weapon Enhancer

Damage: Base: 100 HP, 375% AP per saw.

Effect: N/A

Location: Products

"I SAW what you did there! Get it?"
—AARON

ROCK THROW

Description: A giant boulder drops out of the sky and smashes your enemies. *Boom!*

Category: Offensive

Element: Weapon

Type: Area of Effect (all), Weapon Enhancer

Damage: Base: 100 HP, 750% AP.

Effect: Stuns your enemies.

Location: Products

"Rock on! Heh . . ."
—AXL

ROCK TWISTER

Description: A swirling tornado with rock pieces inside yanks enemies up into the air, damaging and stunning them.

Category: Offensive

Element: Air

Type: Area of Effect (all), Weapon Enhancer

Damage: Base DoT: 50 HP, 200% AP/second.

Effect: Stun your enemies as they land.

Location: Products

ROCKETSHIP

Description: Ready for launch! A rocket takes off from the battlefield, slowing and burning them.

Category: Offensive

Element: Earth

Type: Area of Effect (all), Weapon Enhancer

Damage: Base: 100 HP, 400% AP.

Effect: Slow movement and attack speed of enemies by 15%.

Location: In-store, Extended line

ROCK 'N' ROLL

Description: Sweet guitar riffs can be heard with each strike. Rock on!

Category: Offensive

Element: Sound

Type: Area of Effect (all), Weapon Enhancer

Damage: Base: 25 HP.

Effect: Normal attacks deal 65% more damage.

Location: LEGO.COM, Products

ROLLING FIRE BALL

Description: Surround your knight with a flaming sphere of fire, damaging all who touch it. Explodes at end of duration and burns all enemies who are hit.

Category: Offensive

Element: Fire

Type: Aura

Damage: Base: 50 HP, DoT: 50 HP.

Effect: Burning 50% AP/second, Aura: 100% AP/second.

Location: Products, TV show

ROLLING HEDGEHOG

Description: Spikes stick out of your knight's armor and they can roll around like a hedgehog, dealing damage.

Category: Offensive

Element: Animal

Type: Area of Effect (all), Weapon Enhancer

Damage: Base—Knock Back: 50 HP, 150% AP; Knock Upward: 50 HP, 300% AP.

Effect: N/A

Location: Products

ROTO SENTRY

Description: A "Repeating Bolt thrower" spawns randomly on the battlefield and shoots bolts at the closest enemy.

Category: Offensive

Element: Weapon

Type: Area of Effect (all), Weapon Enhancer

Damage: Base DoT: 25 HP, 150% AP/second.

Effect: N/A

Location: In-store, LEGO.COM

ROYAL BRAWL

Description: Your knight gets increased max health and regeneration per second. Ready to brawl!

Category: Supportive

Element: Armor

Type: Self

Damage: N/A

Effect: Heals your knight for 40% of their max HP. Regenerates 2% of max HP.

Location: LEGO.COM, In-store

RUBBER BAND OF MISCHIEF

Description: Spawn a large rubber band and bounce enemies off if they get too close.

Category: Offensive

Element: Magic

Type: Area of Effect (all), Weapon Enhancer

Damage: Base: 50 HP, 400% AP.

Effect: Knock back your enemies.

Location: LEGO.COM, In-store

RUSHING STRIKE

Description: Charge headfirst toward your enemy and knock them offscreen!
Category: Offensive
Element: Dragon
Type: Area of Effect (all), Weapon Enhancer
Damage: Base: 100 HP, 800% AP.
Effect: Destroys small enemies.
Location: In-store, Products

SABER SLASH

Description: Create a digital saber to slice and dice your enemies.
Category: Offensive
Element: Weapon
Type: Area of Effect (all), Weapon Enhancer
Damage: Base: 50 HP, 300% AP per strike.
Effect: N/A
Location: In-store, TV Show

SAND TORNADO

Description: Summon a tornado that moves toward your enemies and carries them away. Enemies are blinded for five seconds after the tornado drops them.

Category: Offensive

Element: Air

Type: Area of Effect (all), Weapon Enhancer

Damage: Base DoT: 50 HP, 150% AP/second.

Effect: Blinds your enemies.

Location: Extended line, In-store

SEA DRAGON

Description: Wipe out your enemies with a water trail that turns into giant waves!

Category: Offensive

Element: Dragon

Type: Trail

Damage: Base: 100 HP, 625% AP.

Effect: N/A

Location: Products

SEAGULL BOMB

Description: Seagulls swarm the battlefield and drop "bombs" down on your enemies, splattering them from above!

Category: Offensive

Element: Explosion

Type: Area of Effect (all), Weapon Enhancer

Damage: Base: 50 HP, 300% AP. DoT: 25 HP, 150% AP/second.

Effect: Blinds your enemies temporarily.

Location: LEGOLAND

SERPENT OF ANTI VIRUS

Description: Plant a serpent totem in the ground that heals you over time.

Category: Supportive

Element: Animal

Type: Self

Damage: N/A

Effect: Heals your knight for 4% of their max HP.

Location: TV Show, Produccts

SHARK ATTACK

Description: A large pool of water containing a fierce shark appears! The shark's bite instantly destroys smaller enemies and deals great damage to larger ones.

Category: Offensive

Element: Animal

Type: Area of Effect (all), Weapon Enhancer

Damage: Base: 100 HP, 1000% AP to all big enemies nearby.

Effect: On shark bite, swallow all small enemies nearby.

Location: LEGO.COM, Products

SHIELD OF SCHOOLING AND PROTECTION

Description: Create a protective dome around your knight that increases their defense.

Category: Defensive

Element: Bird

Type: Self

Damage: N/A

Effect: Increases your knight's defense by 50%.

Location: TV Show, In-store

SHINING AXE

Description: Sending a huge axe flying into the ground, taking out all enemies in the area.

Category: Offensive

Element: Weapon

Type: Area of Effect (all), Weapon Enhancer

Damage: Base: 50 HP, 125% AP.

Effect: N/A

Location: Products

SHIP WRECKER

Description: A big anchor drags across the screen, damaging stronger enemies and carrying smaller ones away.

Category: Offensive

Element: Water

Type: Area of Effect (all), Weapon Enhancer

Damage: Base: 100 HP, 750% AP to all big enemies.

Effect: Drags all small enemies offscreen.

Location: In-store, Products

SIDEKICK

Description: Your knight strikes with a normal attack and a holographic copy of your knight does the same, but strikes from the opposite direction.

Category: Offensive

Element: Armor

Type: Area of Effect (all), Weapon Enhancer

Damage: N/A

Effect: Your knight's copy strikes from the opposite direction.

Location: In-store, Products

SILK SPIDER

Description: Create a sticky web trap on the ground, trapping baddies. A giant spider falls on your enemies and explodes, dealing damage and poison.

Category: Offensive

Element: Insect

Type: Area of Effect (all), Weapon Enhancer

Damage: Base: 100 HP, 500% AP. DoT: 100% AP poison/second.

Effect: Immobilizes and poisons your enemies.

Location: In-store

SILVER PEGASUS

Description: A majestic, wild Pegasus appears above your knight. Whenever your knight attacks an enemy, they are hurled into the air. When they land, your enemies take damage and drop Memory Bits.

Category: Offensive

Element: Monster

Type: Area of Effect (all), Weapon Enhancer

Damage: Base: 25 HP, 1000% AP.

Effect: Knocks your enemies upward. Enemies drop Memory Bits as they land.

Location: Products

SILVER WHIP

Description: Create a digital whip that whirls around and lashes nearby enemies.

Category: Offensive

Element: Weapon

Type: Area of Effect (all), Weapon Enhancer

Damage: Base: 100 HP, 500% AP per strike.

Effect: Immobilizes your enemies.

Location: In-store, Products

SIR TAUNTALOT

Description: A silly Squirebot wearing a jester's hat appears and taunts all enemies, causing them to chase it around.

Category: Offensive

Element: Weapon

Type: Area of Effect (all), Weapon Enhancer

Damage: N/A

Effect: Taunts your enemies.

Location: Products

SKUNK STENCH

Description: Your knight becomes super stinky, and nearby bad guys can't handle it! They won't attack you for the duration of the Power.

Category: Offensive

Element: Animal

Type: Area of Effect (all), Weapon Enhancer

Damage: N/A

Effect: Your enemies run away, and their movement speed is reduced by 25%.

Location: LEGO Club Magazine, LEGO.COM

SLIME BLAST

Description: Giant balls of goo fall from the sky on random nearby enemies every half second. When they land, they explode and immobilize enemies. Yuck!

Category: Offensive

Element: Poison

Type: Area of Effect (all), Weapon Enhancer

Damage: Base: 50 HP, 125% AP.

Effect: Immobilizes your enemies.

Location: Products

SLIME SLUGS

Description: A helpful snail appears, leaving a slime trail behind which stops enemies and poisons them.

Category: Offensive

Element: Insect

Type: Area of Effect (all), Weapon Enhancer

Damage: Base DoT: 25 HP, 100% AP/second.

Effect: Poisoned enemies are slowed by 25%.

Location: Products

SNAKE DEN

Description: Leave a slithery trap for your enemies on the ground—cobras pop out to menace the baddies.

Category: Offensive

Element: Animal

Type: Area of Effect (all), Weapon Enhancer

Damage: Base: 50 HP, 100% AP per bite. DoT: 50 HP, 75% AP poison/second.

Effect: Poisons your enemies.

Location: LEGO.COM, Products

SNAKESKIN

Description: Snakes!! They stick out of your knight's armor and all of your knight's attacks will deal poison damage as well.

Category: Offensive

Element: Armor

Type: Area of Effect (all), Weapon Enhancer

Damage: Base: 50 HP, 150% AP.

Effect: Poisons your enemies and heals your knight for 4% of their max HP.

Location: In-store

SNAPPER STAND

Description: A huge ball shaped like a turtle shell spawns on the battlefield. Kick it around—after ten bounces, it explodes on the next enemy it hits.

Category: Offensive

Element: Animal

Type: Area of Effect (all), Weapon Enhancer

Damage: Base: 100 HP, 1250% AP explosion damage.

Effect: N/A

Location: In-store, LEGO.COM

SOARING EAGLE

Description: Summon a mighty eagle to assist you, targeting and striking an enemy every two seconds.

Category: Offensive

Element: Bird

Type: Area of Effect (all), Weapon Enhancer

Damage: Base: 50 HP, 300% AP.

Effect: N/A

Location: LEGO.COM, In-store

SOUR STRIKE

Description: Leave a treacherous, poisonous trail behind wherever you go.

Category: Offensive

Element: Poison

Type: Area of Effect (all), Weapon Enhancer

Damage: Base DoT: 50 HP, 175% AP/second.

Effect: Poisons your enemies.

Location: LEGO Club Magazine, LEGO.COM

SPARROW TORNADO

Description: A tornado sweeps across the battlefield, scooping up your enemies. Each time an enemy is sucked into the tornado, a giant sparrow flies out of the tornado and damages all enemies inside.

Category: Offensive

Element: Air

Type: Area of Effect (all), Weapon Enhancer

Damage: Base: 100 HP. Add 50% AP as additional enemies are caught.

Effect: N/A

Location: In-store, Products

SPECIAL DELIVERY

Description: A supply crate lands on the battlefield with a blast! The crate drops a random item.

Category: Offensive

Element: Air

Type: Area of Effect (all), Weapon Enhancer

Damage: Base: 50 HP, 250% AP.

Effect: Drops chicken legs that heal for 15% of max HP and large Memory Bits.

Location: In-store, Products

SPEED ELIXIR

Description: Your knight runs so fast they catch on fire, damaging enemies as you touch them.

Category: Offensive

Element: Fire

Type: Area of Effect (all), Weapon Enhancer

Damage: Base DoT: 25 HP, 150% AP/second.

Effect: Burns and knocks back your enemies. Your knight moves 30% faster.

Location: Merlok 2.0 App

SPIN DRIFTER

Description: Create a swirling elemental vortex of wind and water that slowly draws enemies into it. At the end of its duration, a large wave splashes out of the vortex and flings your enemy into the air.

Category: Offensive

Element: Air

Type: Area of Effect (all), Weapon Enhancer

Damage: Base: 100 HP, 500% AP upon landing.

Effect: Pulls your enemies toward the middle of the vortex and knocks them upward.

Location: In-store, LEGO Club Magazine

SPIRIT FOX

Description: A ghostly spirit fox appears to aid you in battle, swirling around your knight and leaping onto nearby enemies.

Category: Offensive

Element: Animal

Type: Area of Effect (all), Weapon Enhancer

Damage: Base DoT: 50 HP, 400% AP.

Effect: N/A

Location: Products

SPIRIT VORTEX

Description: Summon a vortex of friendly spirits that moves toward your enemies, damaging them and restoring your knight's health.

Category: Offensive

Element: Air

Type: Area of Effect (all), Summoning

Damage: Base DoT: 50 HP, 150% AP/second.

Effect: Restore 20% of the damage dealt by the tornado to your knight.

Location: Products

SQUEEZE WRENCH

Description: A huge wrench appears around an enemy. When your knight runs around the enemy, the wrench tightens and deals damage, ultimately crushing them.

Category: Offensive

Element: Weapon

Type: Area of Effect (all), Weapon Enhancer

Damage: Base: 50 HP, 1000% AP.

Effect: Lure all enemies.

Location: In-store

STAMPEDE

Description: A large bull's head appears over your knight, squashing all enemies.

Category: Offensive

Element: Animal

Type: Area of Effect (all), Weapon Enhancer

Damage: Base: 100 HP, 500% AP.

Effect: Flattens and stuns your enemies.

Location: In-store

STANDING OVATION

Description: A hologram of Lance appears and cheers for you, stunning random monsters with his awesomeness.

Category: Offensive

Element: Light

Type: Area of Effect (all), Weapon Enhancer

Damage: Base: 50 HP, 200% AP.

Effect: Blinds your enemies.

Location: Products

STARFALL

Description: A small star-shaped meteor falls on the enemy, dealing damaging. For each enemy in the zone, another meteor is launched.

Category: Offensive

Element: Fire

Type: Aura

Damage: Base: 50 HP, 100% AP per star.

Effect: N/A

Location: LEGO.COM, TV show

STONE BURST

Description: A giant spike of stone bursts from under the ground, damaging all nearby enemies. If target is stunned, Stone Burst paralyzes them and adds vulnerability.

Category: Offensive

Element: Explosion

Type: Area of Effect (all), Weapon Enhancer

Damage: Base: 100 HP, 500% AP explosion damage to surrounding enemies.

Effect: Stuns your enemies.

Location: In-store, TV Show

STONE STUN

Description: Three stones float around your knight in a circle. If an enemy attacks your knight, they immediately turn to stone!

Category: Defensive

Element: Armor

Type: Self

Damage: N/A

Effect: Petrifies your enemies for eight seconds.

Location: Products

STORM DRAGON

Description: Your knight leaves small orbs of electricity floating behind them. The orbs connect and form an electric arc that shocks your enemies. The orbs then explode, damaging and stunning all enemies they hit.

Category: Offensive

Element: Dragon

Type: Area of Effect (all), Trail

Damage: Base: 50 HP. Orb: Electric Arc damage: 75% AP/second; Orb Explosion damage: 100% AP.

Effect: Stun your enemies for three seconds.

Location: Products

STRIKING BACKLASH

Description: Charge toward your knight's enemies, then zoom back to where you started, striking enemies in your path twice.

Category: Offensive

Element: Electricity

Type: Area of Effect (all), Weapon Enhancer

Damage: Base: 50 HP, 400% AP upon landing.

Effect: Knocks your enemies upward.

Location: TV Show

STRONGHOLD OF RESOLUTION

Description: Smash the ground and create an aura that surrounds your knight. When an enemy enters the aura, a bold hawk emerges from the ground and damages the enemy.

Category: Defensive

Element: Bird

Type: Self

Damage: Base: 50 HP, 275% AP.

Effect: N/A

Location: In-store, Products

STUNNING SHOWMANSHIP

Description: Your knight charges three times in a row, dealing damage to all in their path. Any enemy that is struck becomes stunned.

Category: Offensive

Element: Weapon

Type: Area of Effect (all), Weapon Enhancer

Damage: Base: 50 HP, 200% AP.

Effect: Stuns your enemies.

Location: TV Show

"Ready, Set, Charge!"
—CLAY

SUN FLARE

Description: Shining sun rays burn all enemies surrounding your knight. Hot stuff!

Category: Offensive

Element: Light

Type: Area of Effect (all), Weapon Enhancer

Damage: Base DoT: 25 HP, 100% AP/ second.

Effect: Blinds all enemies.

Location: Products

SUPER HUMAN SPEED

Description: Your knights are invigorated by a green energy that envelops them, cause them to recharge more quickly and move faster on the battlefield.

Category: Supportive

Element: Air

Type: Self (party)

Damage: N/A

Effect: Accelerate recharge rate of Powers by 25%. Your knight moves 40% faster.

Location: Products

SUPERHERO BODYSLAM

Description: Become a SUPER knight and send enemies flying away from you.

Category: Offensive

Element: Magic

Type: Area of Effect (all), Weapon Enhancer

Damage: Base: 50 HP, 25% AP.

Effect: Knocks your enemies upward and stuns them for one second.

Location: TV Show, LEGO.COM

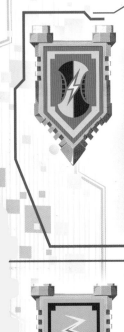

SUPERSONIC SHIELD

Description: Strike the ground and raise a shimmering wall of energy that protects your knights from harm.

Category: Defensive

Element: Electricity

Type: Self

Damage: N/A

Effect: Reflect enemy projectiles and reduce damage by 25%.

Location: In-store, LEGO.COM

SWIFT STING

Description: Launch an energy projectile that bounces between enemies, dealing greater damage with each bounce.

Category: Offensive

Element: Animal

Type: Area of Effect (all), Weapon Enhancer

Damage: Base: 100 HP.

Effect: 10 bounces, 400% AP + 20% AP per bounce.

Location: In-store, Products

SWISS CHEESE

Description: A large hunk of cheese falls from the sky. Shots from within the cheese are fired at baddies, making the cheese Swiss.

Category: Offensive

Element: Food

Type: Area of Effect (all), Weapon Enhancer

Damage: Base: 50 HP, 300% AP.

Effect: Slows enemy movement by 25%.

Location: Products

SWORD OF STRENGTH AND SUPREMACY

Description: A massive sword falls onto the battlefield, piercing the ground and generating a zone around it. While in the zone, your knight's attacks are stronger.

Category: Offensive

Element: Weapon

Type: Area of Effect (all), Weapon Enhancer

Damage: Base: 50 HP.

Effect: Increases damage by 30% and critical damage by 125%.

Location: TV Show, In-store

SWORD TORNADO

Description: Summon a sharp two-bladed sword that spins around your knight, damaging and pushing enemies back.

Category: Offensive

Element: Air

Type: Aura

Damage: Base: 50 HP, 125% AP.

Effect: Pushes your enemies back.

Location: Products

TAKE OFF

Description: Your knight disappears in a puff of feathers and reappears in a random location, bathed in light that restores HP.

Category: Supportive

Element: Bird

Type: Self

Damage: N/A

Effect: Restores 8% of your knight's max HP per second. Pushes back your enemies.

Location: Products

TARGET BLASTER

Description: Call on the digital Powers of Merlok 2.0 to analyze your knight's target, revealing their flaws and making them vulnerable.

Category: Supportive

Element: Explosion

Type: Automatic

Damage: Base: 25 HP.

Effect: Adds vulnerability to the closest enemy. A vulnerable enemy receives 100% more damage from all attacks.

Location: Products

TECH TREE

Description: Tree trunks with branches of lightning grow out of the ground and zap your opponents!

Category: Offensive

Element: Plant

Type: Area of Effect (all), Weapon Enhancer

Damage: Base: 50 HP, 100% AP.

Effect: Absorbing a pack of leaves heals your knight for 1% of max HP.

Location: Products

THUNDER BLAZE

Description: Blind all foes for a short duration and bestow the power of thunder on your knight's weapon.

Category: Supportive

Element: Electricity

Type: Area of Effect (all), Weapon Enhancer

Damage: Base: 25 HP.

Effect: Blinds all your enemies and adds 50% weapon damage as electric damage on each attack.

Location: In-store, Products

TICKING BABOON

Description: Enemies beware! A swinging baboon swoops in and drops ticking bombs.

Category: Offensive

Element: Animal

Type: Area of Effect (all), Weapon Enhancer

Damage: Base: 50 HP, 500% AP.

Effect: N/A

Location: Products

TIMBER!!!

Description: A massive tree trunk appears and falls slowly toward your enemies. When it hits the ground, it rolls away—flattening and damaging all enemies in its path.

Category: Offensive

Element: Plant

Type: Area of Effect (all), Weapon Enhancer

Damage: Base: 200 HP, 2000% AP.

Effect: N/A

Location: In-store

TIME BREACH

Description: Great Scott! Everything around your knight stops moving. Attack enemies at will!

Category: Offensive

Element: Bird

Type: Area of Effect (all), Weapon Enhancer

Damage: N/A

Effect: All enemies are stuck in time.

Location: Products

TITANIUM SWORD

Description: Clay, riding a majestic griffin, flies across the battlefield, attacking enemies as they go. Follows the path you draw across the screen.

Category: Offensive

Element: Weapon

Type: Area of Effect (all), Weapon Enhancer

Damage: Base: 50 HP, 400% AP.

Effect: Sword can only strike enemies once per whirlwind.

Location: Products

"So majestic. Go, Clay!"
—MACY

TOAD

Description: Transform your knight into a big fat frog and pounce on enemies! Three hops and you turn back into a knight.

Category: Offensive

Element: Animal

Type: Area of Effect (all), Weapon Enhancer

Damage: Base: 100 HP, 600% AP.

Effect: N/A

Location: Products

Hop along, froggy!"
—AXL

TONE OF POWER

Description: A clef starts shooting musical notes at your enemies. Each time a note hits an enemy, you can hear sweet music!

Category: Offensive

Element: Sound

Type: Area of Effect (all), Weapon Enhancer

Damage: Base DoT: 10 HP, 100% AP.

Effect: N/A

Location: Products

TOOTH BUSTER

Description: A giant tooth appears on the battlefield and EXPLODES into lots of smaller teeth, which also EXPLODE!

Category: Offensive

Element: Explosion

Type: Area of Effect (all), Weapon Enhancer

Damage: Base (Big Tooth): 50 HP, 500% AP, Base (Small Tooth): 25 HP, 100% AP.

Effect: N/A

Location: Products

TOUCHDOWN

Description: Spike a big football on the battlefield and stun your enemies! Game on!!

Category: Offensive

Element: Armor

Type: Area of Effect (all), Weapon Enhancer

Damage: Base: 150 HP, 1500% AP on elite/boss monsters.

Effect: N/A

Location: Products

TOXIC STING

Description: Summon a scary scorpion to slash and stab at Jestro's minions!

Category: Offensive

Element: Insect

Type: Area of Effect (all), Weapon Enhancer

Damage: Base: 75 HP, 150% AP per attack. DoT: 50 HP. 50% AP/second (poisoned).

Effect: Slows monster movement by 10% and poisons your enemies.

Location: Products, In-store

TRACTOR BEAM

Description: A mysterious force lifts your enemies up into the air and smashes them back down.

Category: Offensive

Element: Weapon

Type: Area of Effect (all), Weapon Enhancer

Damage: Base: 75 HP, 750% AP when landing.

Effect: Holds enemies in the air.

Location: Products, LEGO.COM

TRANSFORMATION

Description: *BAWK!* Transform any monster into a chicken. Reduces monster's HP to the chicken's HP.

Category: Offensive

Element: Bird

Type: Area of Effect (all), Weapon Enhancer

Damage: N/A

Effect: Defeating a chicken drops a chicken leg. Chickens have 100% increased movement speed. Chicken's size and speed are based on the enemy's stats before being transformed.

Location: LEGO.COM, In-store

TRIPLE BACKSTAB

Description: Transports your knight to the three strongest enemies on the battlefield to attack them from behind.

Category: Offensive

Element: Magic

Type: Area of Effect (all), Weapon Enhancer

Damage: Base: 100 HP, 700% AP.

Effect: N/A

Location: Products

TRIPLE HABANERO

Description: Eat one of three habanero chili peppers (yellow, red, or green) and ignite a cone-shaped breath attack that burns enemies!

Category: Offensive

Element: Food

Type: Area of Effect (all), Weapon Enhancer

Damage: Base DoT: 50 HP, 150% AP/second.

Effect: Burns and knocks back your enemies.

Location: In-store

TRIPLE TROUBLE

Description: Summon a ghostly lance to attack three different enemies and knock them back.

Category: Offensive

Element: Weapon

Type: Area of Effect (all), Weapon Enhancer

Damage: Base: 50 HP, 200% AP per triple swing.

Effect: N/A

Location: Products

TURBO KITTY

Description: Your knight becomes super fast and makes cute kitty sounds. *Mew!*

Category: Offensive

Element: Animal

Type: Area of Effect (all), Weapon Enhancer

Damage: N/A

Effect: Your knight moves 100% faster.

Location: TV Show

ULTRA ARMOR ACTIVATE

Description: Surround your knight with a protective dome of electricity. Enemies who attack get zapped by electricity. *YOW!*

Category: Defensive

Element: Electricity

Type: Self

Damage: Base: 100 HP, Bounce: 50 HP. 175% AP when attacked. 125% AP on each target per bounce.

Effect: 15% damage reduction.

Location: TV Show, In-store

ULTRA ARMOR AWESOME SAUCE

Description: Three floating orbs of energy appear around your knight. When your knight is hit, an orb is consumed and heals your knight.

Category: Supportive

Element: Electricity

Type: Trigger

Damage: N/A

Effect: Health 10% of your knight's max HP when hit.

Location: LEGO.COM, In-store

UNDER WOE

Description: *ACK!* Underwear falls from the sky on random enemies. When hit, an enemy shrinks by 50%, reducing movement speed and damage.

Category: Offensive

Element: Armor

Type: Area of Effect (all), Weapon Enhancer

Damage: N/A

Effect: Underwear falls every second on a nearby enemy. Enemies struck by underwear deal 50% less damage and move 50% slower for five seconds.

Location: LEGO Club Magazine, LEGOLAND

VEIL OF CONCEALMENT

Description: Turns your knight invisible; their next attack deals massive damage.

Category: Offensive

Element: Animal

Type: Area of Effect (all), Weapon Enhancer

Damage: Base: 100 HP, 2500% normal attack damage when breaking stealth to attack.

Effect: Your knight becomes invisible.

Location: Books, Products

VENOM BITE

Description: Two huge poison bombs drop on enemies every second. Take that!

Category: Offensive

Element: Poison

Type: Area of Effect (all), Weapon Enhancer

Damage: Base: 100 HP, DoT: 25 HP. 125% AP upon landing.

Effect: Poisons your enemies at 25% AP/second.

Location: Products

VERTIGO

Description: Open a black hole in the ground for enemies to fall into, maybe for eternity! Nah, they just fall from the sky and crash back into the ground.

Category: Offensive

Element: Air

Type: Area of Effect (all), Weapon Enhancer

Damage: Base: 100 HP, 1500% AP.

Effect: N/A

Location: Merlok 2.0 App, In-store

> *"Don't look down!"*
> —AVA

WALL BLOCK

Description: Slam the ground and a protective wall of stone rises in front of your knight.

Category: Defensive

Element: Earth

Type: Self

Damage: N/A

Effect: Splits the screen in half, blocking ranged attacks and your enemy's movement.

Location: Products

WASP MISSILE

Description: Every two seconds, a wasp-shaped projectile launches toward your enemies and explodes! Quick, get the bug spray!

Category: Offensive

Element: Insect

Type: Area of Effect (all), Weapon Enhancer

Damage: Base: 50 HP, DoT: 50 HP, 300% AP.

Effect: 50% chance to poison enemies, dealing an additional 50% AP/second.

Location: In-store, Products

WATER WALL

Description: Whoa! A giant wave of water sloshes in from one side of the screen, damaging and moving all enemies to the other side.

Category: Offensive

Element: Water

Type: Area of Effect (all), Weapon Enhancer

Damage: Base: 100 HP, 750% damage to all enemies.

Effect: Push all enemies to the left or right end of the screen.

Location: In-store, LEGO.COM

WEDGIE OF DOOM

Description: The ultimate wedgie. All enemies get pulled up into the air and dropped back down again. Harsh!

Category: Offensive

Element: Armor

Type: Area of Effect (all), Weapon Enhancer

Damage: Base DoT: 25 HP, 100% AP/ second.

Effect: Confuses your enemies.

Location: TV Show

WHIPLASH

Description: A whip materializes over each enemy and lashes them once. *Snap!*

Category: Offensive

Element: Weapon

Type: Area of Effect (all), Weapon Enhancer

Damage: N/A

Effect: Reduces enemy damage by 50%.

Location: Extended line, LEGO.COM

WHIRLWIND

Description: Summon an epic whirlwind made of axes to chop your enemies to tiny bits.

Category: Offensive

Element: Air

Type: Area of Effect (all), Weapon Enhancer

Damage: Base DoT: 50 HP, 175% AP/second.

Effect: Pulls enemies toward the center of the whirlwind.

Location: Products

WILD BOAR

Description: Invoke the power of a mighty boar to improve your knight's movement speed and offense.

Category: Offensive

Element: Animal

Type: Area of Effect (all), Weapon Enhancer

Damage: Base: 25 HP.

Effect: Increases movement speed by 20%, damage from normal attacks by 3% and critical damage by 25%.

Location: In-store, LEGO.COM

WRECKING BALL

Description: Draw a trail on the ground that your knight follows, swinging a wrecking ball as he or she goes. Great for dealing with enemies scattered on the battlefield.

Category: Offensive

Element: Weapon

Type: Area of Effect (all), Weapon Enhancer

Damage: Base: 50 HP, 300% AP per hit.

Effect: Knocks back your enemies.

Location: Products

YETI SNEEZE

Description: Goo balls fly on-screen and land on the ground with a slime blast. Gross!

Category: Offensive

Element: Water

Type: Area of Effect (all), Weapon Enhancer

Damage: Base: 50 HP, 200% AP.

Effect: Slows enemy movement by 30%.

Location: Products

ZAP ZAP

Description: Four lightning traps are set around your knight. When the traps are sprung, enemies are paralyzed and take lightning damage.

Category: Offensive

Element: Electricity

Type: Area of Effect (all), Weapon Enhancer

Damage: Base: 50 HP, 600% AP.

Effect: Paralyzes your enemies.

Location: LEGO Club Magazine, Products

Forbidden Powers

Forbidden Powers are the most dangerous, terrible, and destructive Powers in all of Knighton! Using them could result in harm to others and worse, yourself! Consider yourself warned—Jestro and Monstrox want these for a reason, and it's not to conjure puppies. These Powers were outlawed by the Wizards' Council because they're extremely dangerous. If you come across them, leave them be!

AGING ANTILIFE

Description: Launch a deadly ray that sucks the life out of anything it touches.

Category: Offensive

Element: Magic

Type: Area of Effect (all), Weapon Enhancer

Damage: N/A

Effect: All enemies lose 8% of their remaining HP and movement speed/second. Your knight is healed for 10% of the damage dealt with this Power.

Location: Books

AWESOME ANNIHILATION

Description: "The most evil Forbidden Power of all—do not use this under any circumstances!! You could destroy everything. I've already said too much! Good thing these pesky Forbidden Powers are under lock and key."
—Merlok 2.0

Category: Offensive

Element: Explosion

Type: Area of Effect (all), Weapon Enhancer

Damage: Base: 50 HP, 500% AP explosion damage.

Effect: N/A

Location: TV Show

BLAZING BURN

Description: Summon an evil-looking fire to the center of the battlefield. Enemies standing too close to the fire will take damage. The evil fire spawns smaller fires that jump toward your enemies and explode—*yow!*

Category: Offensive

Element: Fire

Type: Area of Effect (all), Weapon Enhancer

Damage: Base DoT: Big Fire—25 HP, 100% AP/second. Small Fire—50 HP, 300% AP.

Effect: N/A

Location: TV Show

COLLAPSING CRUMBLE

Description: Large pillars appear on the battlefield, and when your enemies collide with them, they shake and then crumble!

Category: Offensive

Element: Earth

Type: Area of Effect (all), Weapon Enhancer

Damage: Base: 100 HP, 1000% AP.

Effect: N/A

Location: TV Show

CORRUPTING CRUSH

Description: Giant cracks tear open the ground and lava comes bubbling out, burning all enemies nearby!

Category: Offensive

Element: Earth

Type: Area of Effect (all), Weapon Enhancer

Damage: Base DoT: 50 HP, 250% AP/second.

Effect: N/A

Location: Products

"I love crushing things!"
—MONSTROX

DEVASTATING DECAY

Description: Translucent maggots appear (yuck!) and eat away life.

Category: Offensive

Element: Food

Type: Area of Effect (all), Weapon Enhancer

Damage: Base DoT: 50 HP, 175% AP/second.

Effect: Poisons your enemies. Defeating an enemy spawns a small chicken leg that heals your knight for 5% of their max HP.

Location: Products

DEVIOUS DEMOLITION

Description: Six explosions converge on the middle of the battlefield, triggering a single massive explosion!

Category: Offensive

Element: Explosion

Type: Area of Effect (all), Weapon Enhancer

Damage: Base: Small Explosion—25 HP, 300% AP, Big Explosion—75 HP, 800% AP.

Effect: N/A

Location: TV Show

DREADFUL DISINTEGRATION

Description: Deals massive damage to the enemy closest to your knight as they begin to disintegrate!

Category: Offensive

Element: Magic

Type: Area of Effect (all), Weapon Enhancer

Damage: Base DoT: 50 HP, 400% AP/second.

Effect: N/A

Location: LEGO.COM

EVIL EVAPORATE

Description: Summon a pernicious potion that releases an evil spirit, which attacks and bites your enemies. Both spirit and potion evaporate at the end of the Power's duration.

Category: Offensive

Element: Poison

Type: Area of Effect (all), Weapon Enhancer

Damage: Base: 50 HP, 250% AP per strike.

Effect: N/A

Location: TV Show

HORRIBLE HUNGER

Description: SNAKES! Snakes slither toward random enemies every second and bite them with sharp, pointy teeth. When the Power has ended, your knight is healed.

Category: Offensive

Element: Animal

Type: Area of Effect (all), Weapon Enhancer

Damage: Base: 50 HP, 150% AP.

Effect: Heals your knight for 2% of their max HP as a snake returns to them.

Location: Products

MALICIOUS MELTING

Description: A bubbling hot lava pool appears, catching unsuspecting enemies by surprise!

Category: Offensive

Element: Fire

Type: Area of Effect (all), Weapon Enhancer

Damage: Base DoT: 50 HP, 175% AP.

Effect: Slows enemy movement and attack by 25%.

Location: Products, TV Show

METAL MORPHOSIS

Description: Your enemies are petrified and turned into metal! Gnarly!

Category: Offensive

Element: Weapon

Type: Area of Effect (all), Weapon Enhancer

Damage: N/A

Effect: Slows enemies by 100% over three seconds, then petrifies them.

Location: TV Show

RAVAGING ROT

Description: A basket of rotten apples appears on the battlefield! Apples pop out and splatter on the ground, creating a gross puddle of poisoned apple juice.

Category: Offensive

Element: Food

Type: Area of Effect (all), Weapon Enhancer

Damage: Base DoT: 50 HP, 125% AP/second.

Effect: Enemies in puddle are slowed 50%. Knight in puddle is healed for 2% of their max HP.

Location: TV Show

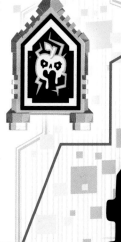

RELENTLESS RUST

Description: Causes your enemies to slow down and rust like old machinery.

Category: Offensive

Element: Armor

Type: Area of Effect (all), Weapon Enhancer

Damage: N/A

Effect: Enemy movement is slowed by 40%, and enemies take 75% more damage from your knight's attacks.

Location: TV Show

SCREAMING SHATTER

Description: A horrifying shriek shocks your enemies, massively reducing their damage.

Category: Offensive

Element: Weapon

Type: Area of Effect (all), Weapon Enhancer

Damage: N/A

Effect: Reduce the damage dealt by enemies to zero.

Location: LEGO.COM

SHOCKING SCARE

Description: Lightning streaks down from the sky, striking fear into your enemies!

Category: Offensive

Element: Magic

Type: Area of Effect (all), Weapon Enhancer

Damage: Base: 75 HP, 400% AP.

Effect: Stuns your enemies.

Location: TV Show

THUNDERING THRASH

Description: Your knight is imbued with the power of lightning, dealing damage to all surrounding enemies!

Category: Offensive

Element: Monster

Type: Area of Effect (all), Weapon Enhancer

Damage: Base: 25 HP (spark), 100% AP (spark).

Effect: Every three sparks, stuns your enemies for one second.

Location: Products

VICIOUS VOLTAGE

Description: "Send fierce electric currents out and short-circuit anything electrical (and I mean anything!)."
—Merlok 2.0

Category: Offensive

Element: Air

Type: Area of Effect (all), Weapon Enhancer

Damage: Base: 50 HP, 200% AP for each bolt.

Effect: N/A

Location: Books

VOLCANIC VENGEANCE

Description: A volcano erupts on the battlefield, damaging both the enemies and your knight! Try to push baddies into the lava and toast them.

Category: Offensive

Element: Fire

Type: Area of Effect (all), Weapon Enhancer

Damage: Base: 50 HP, 400% AP.

Effect: Stuns your enemies.

Location: Merlok 2.0 App

"Should I get volcano insurance?"
—JESTRO

WRECKING WRATH

Description: An evil wraith bites your enemies! Good thing it's chained to the ground—who knows what could happen?

Category: Offensive

Element: Weapon

Type: Area of Effect (all), Weapon Enhancer

Damage: Base: 50 HP, 300% AP.

Effect: N/A

Location: Products

COMBO
NEXO
Powers

With support from Merlok 2.0, Robin and Ava have developed a new way for you to wield NEXO Powers! They're calling it COMBO NEXO Powers, and they could be the difference between victory and defeat for a knight on the battlefield.

This is how it works: Three knights must form together to download a COMBO NEXO Power. Once the Power has charged up completely, the three knights now have the power to challenge and defeat large and terrifying monsters like the Rockliths.

They're confident that the triple-knight download interface is functioning as intended, and they'd like you to begin beta testing it for them. Don't worry, it's stable—and it will serve you well on the battlefield. They've squashed all the bugs out with extensive testing.

Now go and combine your powers!

NEXO Suits and COMBO NEXO Suit Powers

Robin has been hard at work refining his mech design here at the Fortrex, and has come up with a smaller, more high-tech version that we are calling the NEXO Battle Suits. These are similar to the mechs used by Robin and the king, and are stuffed with cool tech.

The coolest thing about the new NEXO Suits, though, is that they enable only one knight to use a Combo Power, instead of the usual three knights required to activate a Combo Power. That's right—this suit packs three times the Power! You can use these powerful, uh, Powers to battle massive monsters like Rockliths and turn them to dust!

Now here's another cool thing you should know: Three mechs together can download the

Ultimate COMBO NEXO Power —three Combo Powers together that are a perfect match. This Ultimate Power can be used to destroy any monsters that are infused with a Forbidden Power. This is very important, because those monsters would be difficult, if not impossible, to defeat otherwise! Mechs are the key to success here. They are engineered specifically to channel these special powers for maximum damage. Use them to your advantage and hunt down Jestro's minions!

Conclusion

Remember, knights-in-training, that you can share NEXO Powers with your friends using the Merlok 2.0 app. You never know when you might stumble upon a new NEXO Power, so be sure to keep notes in the back of this pocket guide to help keep track of them. Plus: We've added a few bonus Powers in the back for you to practice with! Happy hunting!

BAD REPUTATION

Description: Summon a big thumb and squish your enemies!
Category: Offensive
Element: Magic
Type: Area of Effect
Damage: Base: 25 HP, 100% AP.
Effect: Flatten and stun enemies.
Location: Books

LIGHT BURST

Description: Throw light projectiles around your enemies to confuse them and damage them.
Category: Offensive
Element: Explosion
Type: Area of Effect
Damage: Base: 75 HP, 750% AP.
Effect: Blind your enemies with sparkles!
Location: Books

SHADOW SNAIL

Description: Slows down enemies and makes them vulnerable by pouring ink on them.

Category: Offensive

Element: Animal

Type: Area of Effect

Damage: Base: 100 HP, 375% AP.

Effect: Affected enemies in black ink.

Location: Books

TIC-TAC-TOE

Description: Summon a tic-tac-toe board to damage enemies.

Category: Offensive

Element: Weapon

Type: Area of Effect/Weapon enhancer

Damage: Base: 25 HP, 200% AP.

Effect: Damages enemies with a tic-tac-toe board.

Location: Books

NOTES

~~#~~

1000 SHADOW

Snail tic-tac

TOE

Bad

NOTES

NOTES

NOTES

NOTES

NOTES

NOTES

NOTES

NOTES